Horizons

Spelling and Vocabulary

Teacher's Guide

Author:
Mary Ellen Quint, Ph.D.

Editor:
Alan Christopherson, M.S.

Graphic Design:
Jennifer L. Davis, B.S.

Illustration:
Alpha Omega Creative Services

Alpha Omega Publications, Inc. • Rock Rapids, IA

© MMI by Alpha Omega Publications, Inc.® All rights reserved.
804 N. 2nd Ave. E., Rock Rapids, IA 51246-1759

Printed in the United States of America

ISBN 978-0-7403-0218-3

Spelling and Vocabulary 2

Teacher's Guide

Contents

Introduction

Introduction

"Whatever you do, work at it with all your heart, as working for the Lord, not for men."
(Colossians 3:23).

Approaches to Spelling have changed over the years from simple rote memorization of words, often outside any context, to an integrated study of words in relation to their use in the language. Spelling programs, today, move in many directions. Most present some selection of words to be studied, memorized, and used in a written context. Others present guidelines for approaching spelling, but leave the choice of words to the teacher who must then determine which words the students need to know how to spell for successful completion of writing assignments and the study of individual subjects. Whichever approach is taken, most programs agree that words must be studied within the context of the language and that words must be used in a written context.

Horizons Spelling Program Features

The Horizons Spelling program presents word lists chosen from lists of most frequently used words, sight words, and words chosen for particular phonetic or rhyming patterns. Each lesson also supplies space for three additional "working words"—words chosen by the teacher or parent that apply to the student's experience with words. These "working words" can be taken from other subject areas or chosen on an individual basis from words frequently used, but misspelled, in the student's daily writing.

The program is divided into 160 lessons that can be covered in a 32-week period of time, an average of 5 lessons per week. Each week's lessons include 20 spelling words. Four review units are spread through the year at weeks 8, 16, 24, and 32. This division should accommodate classroom schedules for the school year. Home schooling schedules, which are more flexible, may choose to take more or less time depending on the student's progress.

A Spelling Dictionary is provided for the spelling words. This dictionary is presented as a separate volume from the Spelling text so that the students may use it more easily and avoid having to move back and forth from the lesson to the back of the book. Space is also provided at the end of the dictionary for the "working words" selected for each week. Students enter their words in the dictionary each week, writing them under the appropriate letter of the alphabet.

The Spelling Dictionary and this Teacher's Guide also contain a cumulative word list from Horizons Spelling Grades 1 and 2.

Weekly Schedule

The approach used to teach words for the week is:

Day 1: Assess student's knowledge and introduce words

Day 2: Examine and explore words

Day 3: Look at context and meaning of words

Day 4: Apply understanding of words in writing

Day 5: Assess and evaluate progress

The Horizons Spelling Program provides pages for assessment within the context of the week's lessons. The first page of each new set of lessons is entitled "What Do You Know?" The last page of each set is for testing, correction, and practice.

"What Do You Know?"

This page is a simple assessment tool to see what children already know about the spelling words for the week. It is **NOT** used as a **PRE-TEST**. No grades are kept.

The words for the week are said aloud by the teacher, repeated in the context of a sentence, then repeated again.

1. The students write each word as they think it is spelled on the lines in the first column.

2. When all words have been given, the teacher then looks at the column of words and writes the corrections for misspelled words in the second column. This process is extremely important for the following reasons:

   • It gives the teacher an insight into the student's understanding of words and sounds.

   • It gives the teacher an early indication of problems, such as reversals of letters.

   • It also gives the teacher an opportunity to work with the student, complimenting all efforts and correctly spelled words (or even parts of words), encouraging the student, and helping the student approach the spelling of unknown words.

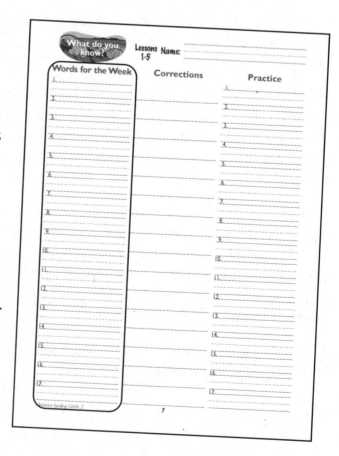

3. The students then practice writing the corrected words in the **Practice** column.

4. The second side of the page provides the student's first "official" look at the words for the week. Go over the words one by one. Introduce the working words of choice for the week.

5. Help the students to write two sentences using some of the words for the week. This may be done initially as a class project in which one sentence is written on the board for the entire class to copy, but it should move to the point where students can write their own sentences.

6. Practice space is given for all the spelling words including the working words chosen for the week.

This second page may be used as extra in-class work or sent home as a study guide.

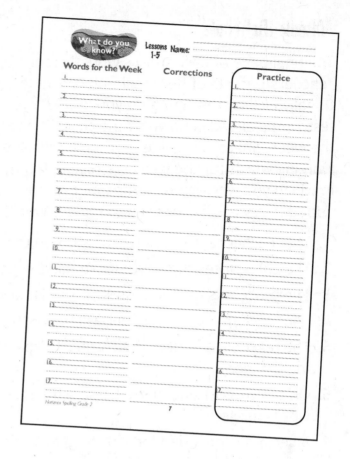

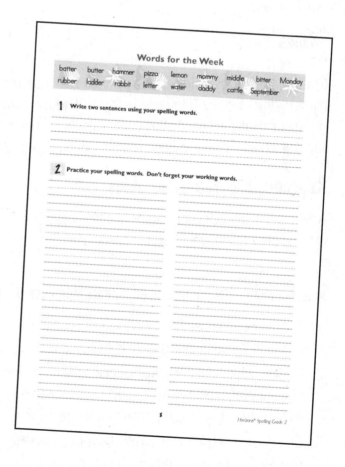

"Check-Up Time"

The final page of each week's work (Lessons 5, 10, 15, 20, 25, etc.) is an assessment page. Teachers/parents of home schoolers can decide what will be assessed. If a child did exceptionally well on the "What do you know?" pre-assessment, the teacher may choose not to test words already known by the child. The teacher may also choose to test all words for the week. Space is provided for the word list given, but make sure that the two "choice" working words for the week are tested. It may be wise to keep a notebook on each child in which you will record words that present particular difficulties. These words could be added to review lists or used to replace words already mastered in a review unit.

1. The teacher says the word, repeats it in the context of a sentence, then repeats the word.

2. The child writes the word dictated in the **Spelling Test** column.

3. The process is repeated until all words have been tested.

4. The teacher may correct in class by writing the words on the board.

5. The teacher then uses the correction space provided to write any corrections for words misspelled.

6. On the second side of the Lesson, the student practices the correct spelling of any words missed.

7. A section is provided for retesting, for testing additional sight or "working words" added for the week, and for additional practice.

"Rules"

Spelling/phonics rules that apply to the lessons are included in the handbook rather than in the student book. They are listed in the individual lessons, but are also found in reproducible masters that can be enlarged for bulletin board use or copied to make individual "rule books" for the children. Go over the rules with the children at the beginning of each week's lesson.

Reproducible Teaching Aids

Additional practice worksheets are also included as reproducible masters. There is one worksheet for each week. These may be used in class or as homework assignments.

Materials for Extended Practice and Activities

1. A practice sheet for each week is included as a reproducible master. It may be used in class or as a homework assignment.

2. In Spelling 1, the students compiled notebooks of word families. If these notebooks are still available, have the students use them as a resource and add to them. If they are not available, new pages/charts can be made for the word families encountered in the units.

3. Classroom charts of word families can be made and posted to help the students see the relationships between words.

4. Have a spelling notebook for each student. In this notebook, they will have two sections: (1) they will write sentences for all of their spelling words each week; (2) they will write definitions for all of their "choice" working words for the week. These two weekly activities may be done in class or as homework. Since each lesson has 20 words, have the students divide their sentence writing over several days; i.e., 4 sentences per day for 5 days; 5 sentences per day for 4 days; and so on. When the activities in the Spelling book include writing sentences, the number in the notebook is reduced. The definitions of "choice" words should be done early in the week. Check the notebooks weekly, commenting on the good points and providing additional practice for those words and English skills that need reinforcement.

5. A Language Arts or Spelling Learning Center can be created in the room. Materials can include:

   • At least two sets of flash cards of the spelling words for the week: one set of complete words, one set in which the words are divided into syllables.

   • Word family pages for the week's words with blank pages to add new words.

   • A scrabble-type game to encourage spelling of new words.

   • Story starters for each week's lessons. These can be made using pictures from magazines or other sources. Look for pictures that include some of the spelling words for the week. Mount the pictures on cards and keep in a folder. Have lined paper available so that the students can go to the center, choose a picture, and write about it. Pictures are then returned to the folders when the student finishes the story.

   • A set of alphabet cards and a cumulative set of spelling word cards to be used for practicing dividing words into the correct ABC order.

Spelling Dictionary

The *Spelling Dictionary* is an integral part of the Horizons Spelling Program and accomplishes several purposes:

1. Students will become acquainted with the format and function of a simple dictionary.

2. Students will learn the function of guide words and diacritical markings.

3. Students will be able to see and read their spelling words within the context of a sentence.

4. Students will have an opportunity to practice their alphabetizing and reading/writing skills by using the *Spelling Dictionary* to perform the following tasks:

   • Look up the spelling words at the beginning of each week's lessons.

   • Record their weekly "working words" in the appropriate location at the back of the *Spelling Dictionary*.

   • Use the *Spelling Dictionary* as a resource for writing sentences and stories.

Parts of speech are identified, and plural and comparative forms of words are also shown.

Word Family Charts and Notebooks

Word families involve words that have the same phonogram. If the families are based on the ending sound the words in each family will rhyme. Some of the most common word families in English are: -ab, -ack, -ag, -ail, -ain, -ake, -ale, -all, -am, -an, -ank, -ap, -ash, -at, -ate, -aw, -ay, -eat, -ed, -eed, -ell, -est, -ew, -ice, -ick, -ide, -ight, -ill, -im, -in, -ine, -ing, -ink, -ip, -it, -ob, -ock, -oke, -op, -ore, -ot, -out, -ow, -uck, -ug, -um, -unk, -y.

Skilled readers recognize patterns in words and rather than sound out a word letter by letter will decode new words based on predictable patterns that they already know. If a student can read the word cat then it is very likely that he/she will be able to read other –at words like sat, mat, flat, pat, splat, hat, that, brat, or chat. These words all have the same chunks or rimes as the word ending.

Word families can also be based on the vowel sound, on the initial consonant sound, or on other categories of similarity. The student will get additional exposure to the words as he/she sorts and classifies them into these groups.

To extend and enhance the learning of each week's word list the teacher's notes for this course suggest that word family charts be made that can be posted in the classroom. This will be an ongoing process in which words will be added to each category as they are introduced in the course. To further extend this process, the student should compile a notebook or notebooks of word families. These notebooks can be used as a resource for the next grade level and the student can add new words to them as they are introduced.

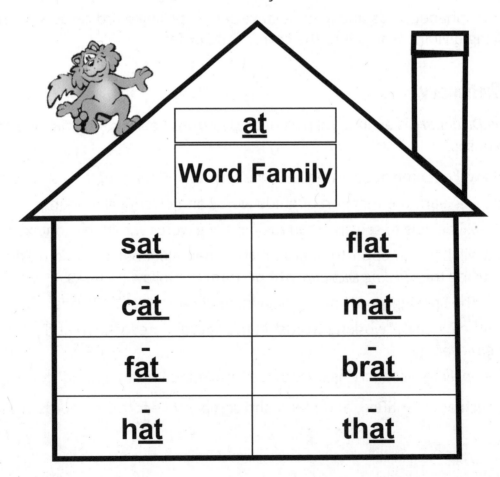

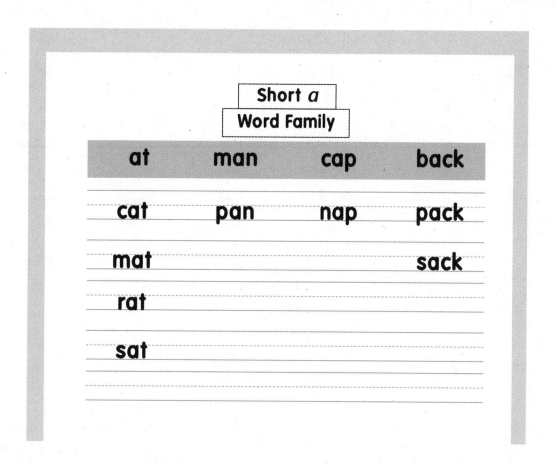

Short *a* Word Family			
at	man	cap	back
cat	pan	nap	pack
mat			sack
rat			
sat			

Penmanship

The student workbooks have perforated pages so the lesson sheets can be removed from the book for the student. Removing the pages is essential to promoting good penmanship. It will be impossible for the student to write neatly on the pages if they are only folded back on the binding of the book. The raised edge of the center binding of the book will prohibit the student's hand from holding a consistent position as they write across the page. After the lesson pages have been completed, they can be punched and stored in a 3-ring binder. Completed lessons can be used for drill, review, and preparation for the test.

Although this course is not a formal penmanship program, guidelines have been provided on all of the student pages to promote good penmanship. A letter formation guide is provided in both the Teacher's Guide and the Student Workbook. This guide can be followed or if you wish, another style can be used.

Correct Formation of Manuscript Letters and Numbers

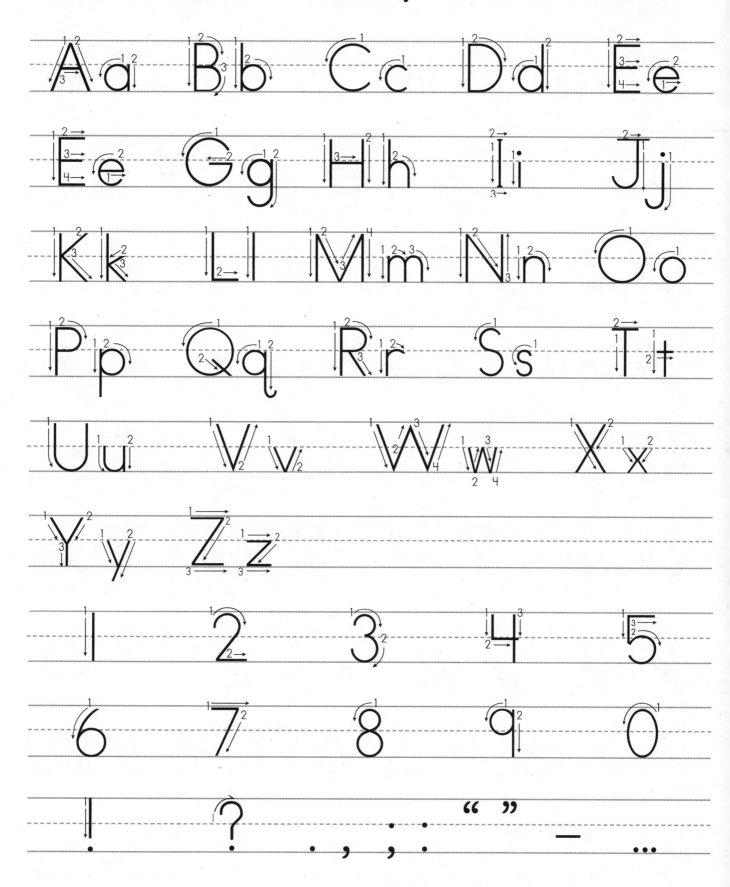

Correct Formation of Cursive Letters and Numbers

Aa Bb Cc Dd

Ee Ff Gg Hh

Ii Jj Kk Ll

Mm Nn Oo Pp

Qq Rr Ss Tt

Uu Vv Ww Xx

Yy Zz

1 2 3 4 5 6 7 8 9 10

! ? . , : ; " " — ...

Scope & Sequence

Week 1

Lessons 1-5:

Goal: To review and study initial, medial, and final consonant sounds. To review division of words into syllables.

Week 2

Lessons 6-10:

Goal: To learn to recognize and spell words with the short ă, ĭ, and ŭ sounds.

Week 3

Lessons 11-15:

Goal: To recognize and spell words with short ŏ and ĕ sounds.

Week 4

Lessons 16-20:

Goal: To recognize and spell words with long ā, ī, and ū sounds.

Week 5

Lessons 21-25:

Goal: To recognize and spell words with the long ō and long ē sound.

Week 6

Lessons 26-30:

Goal: To recognize and spell compound words.

Week 7

Lessons 31-35:

Goal: To recognize and spell words with **r** blends. To recognize and spell words using **y** as a consonant/vowel.

Week 8

Lessons 36-40:

Goal: To review words from Lessons 1–35. Review the rules for the first seven weeks.

Week 9

Lessons 41-45:

Goal: To recognize and spell words with the consonant digraphs **sh**, **ch**, **wh**, and **th**.

Week 10

Lessons 46-50:

Goals: To recognize contractions and the words they represent.

Week 11

Lessons 51-55:

Goal: To recognize and spell the plurals of words ending in **-s**, **-es**. To recognize and spell correctly the plural of words ending in **-fe**.

Week 12

Lessons 56-60:

Goal: To recognize and spell correctly words ending with the suffixes **-ful**, **-less**, and **-ment**.

Week 13

Lessons 61-65:

Goal: To recognize and spell words ending in **-ing**, **-ong**, **-ung**, and **-ang**.

Week 14

Lessons 66-70:

Goal: To recognize and spell words having the hard and soft **c** sounds. To recognize and spell words having the hard and soft **g** sounds.

Week 15

Lessons 71-75:

Goal: To recognize and spell words having the long and short **oo** (u̇ and ü) sounds.

Week 16

Lessons 76-80:

Goal: To review words from Lessons 41–75. Review all rules used in the last seven weeks.

Week 17

Lessons 81-85:

Goal: To recognize and spell words with the **ow** (clown), **ow** (low) and **ou** sounds.

Week 18

Lessons 86-90:

Goal: To recognize the different spellings of the **er** sound in words (**er, ir, ur, wor, ear**).

Week 19

Lessons 91-95:

Goal: To recognize and spell words with **s** blends.

Week 20

Lessons 96-100:

Goal: To recognize and spell homophones.

Week 21

Lessons 101-105:

Goal: To recognize and spell words with the **k** sound of **qu** and **ch**.

Week 22

Lessons 106-110:

Goal: To recognize and spell words with silent letters **gn**, **kn**, and **sc**. To recognize and spell the **z** sound of **s**.

Week 23

Lessons 111-115:

Goal: To recognize and spell comparative words ending in **-er** and **-est**.

Week 24

Lessons 116-120:

Goal: To review spelling words from Lessons 81–115. Review all rules used in the last seven weeks.

Week 25

Lessons 121-125:

Goal: To recognize and spell the possessive form of words ending in **-s** and **'s**. To recognize and spell the **k** sound of **ck**.

Week 26

Lessons 126-130:

Goal: To recognize and spell words with **l** blends.

Week 27

Lessons 131-135:

Goal: To recognize and spell irregular plurals. To recognize and spell words ending in **-x** and **-xes**.

Week 28

Lessons 136-140:

Goal: To recognize and spell the three different sounds of the ending **-ed**.

Week 29

Lessons 141-145:

Goal: To recognize and spell number words.

Week 30

Lessons 146-150:

Goal: To recognize and spell words ending in **-le**.

Week 31

Lessons 151-155:

Goal: To recognize and spell words with the prefixes **un-** and **en-**.

Week 32

Lessons 156-160:

Goal: To review spelling words from Lessons 117–155. Review all spelling rules.

Teacher Lessons

Week 1

Lessons 1-5 - Assess Student's Knowledge

Goal: To review and study initial, medial, and final consonant sounds. To review division of words into syllables.

1. Review:

   Vowels: **a**, **e**, **i**, **o**, **u**, and sometimes **y**.

   Consonants: all the other letters of the alphabet, and usually, **y**.

2. Review **rules for syllables**:

   A one-syllable word is never divided.

   Many words are made of small parts called syllables. Each syllable has one vowel sound.

   (See additional rules for syllables in the "Reproducible Phonics Rules Flashcards" section in this Teacher's Guide.)

What Do You Know?

Give the students the What do you know? page for Lessons 1–5 from the Student Workbook. Tell them that this page will be used to see what they already know about the words for the week. Ask them to listen carefully to each word as you say it, repeat it in a sentence, and say it once again. Follow the procedures for this page as described in the *Introduction* at the beginning of this Teacher's Guide.

Ask the children to write their working words for the week in the word box and on their own paper.

Show the children how to write their Working Words in the appropriate section at the back of their *Spelling Dictionary*.

What do you know?
Lessons 1-5   Name: _____

Words for the Week	Corrections	Practice
batter		
rubber		
butter		
ladder		
hammer		
rabbit		
pizza		
letter		
lemon		
water		
mommy		
daddy		
middle		
cattle		
bitter		
September		
Monday		

Horizons Spelling Grade 2   7

Week 1: Syllables

Many words are made of small parts called syllables. Each syllable has one vowel sound.

A one-syllable word is never divided.

154   *Horizons® Spelling Grade 2*

Lesson 1 - Introduce Words

Activities:

1. Give the students Lesson 1.

2. Ask them what they notice about MOST of the words on their word list for the week. (Possible observations: double consonants in the middle; two-syllable words)

3. Review the words with the students.

4. **Activity 1:** Tell the students that they will be looking at the words and grouping them by the double MIDDLE consonants. Do the first few together and have the students complete independently as they are able.

5. **Activity 2:** Write the working words chosen for the week on the board. Ask the students to write all 5 of their working words for the week on the lines provided.

6. **Activity 3:** Students will write their working words in their Spelling dictionaries in the back section. Words are to be written under the correct letter of the alphabet.

7. Remember that all pages should be removed from the Student Workbook to promote good penmanship.

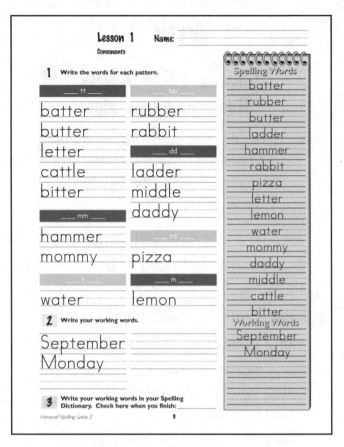

Extended Activities for the Week:

1. Send a list of the week's words home for further study. You may want to include a letter to the parents urging them to help the student both study and use the words for each week. Emphasize the importance of using spelling words in sentences, in speech, in stories, etc., so that they are given a context and not simply memorized in isolation.

2. Assign reproducible *Week 1 Worksheet* either as homework or as an added classroom activity.

3. Have students write the definitions of the "choice" working words in their notebooks.

4. Have the students begin the writing of sentences for each spelling word in their notebooks.

Lesson 2 - Examine and Explore Words

Teaching Tips:

1. Review the rules for the week. (See the **Reproducible Phonics Rules Flashcards** at the end of this Teacher's Guide.)
2. Review the week's words in the box at the top of Lesson 2.

Activities:

1. Give the students Lesson 2.
2. Review the words in the word box and the working words for the week.
3. **Activity 1:** Read the directions with the students. Ask them to draw a line from the clue in the first column to the spelling word in the second column that is described by the clue. This may be done together or independently, depending on the ability of the students.
4. **Activity 2:** Have the students read the directions and complete the assignment.
5. **Activity 3:** As a preparation for this assignment, review ABC order with the students. Do a few simple exercises on the board demonstrating the arrangement of words in ABC order by first letter. Write the following words on the board: **lemon, mommy, bitter, rabbit.**

   Ask the students to arrange them in ABC order: **bitter, lemon, mommy, rabbit.**

   Remind the students that if all the words begin with the same letter or letters, they must look to the second letter to arrange the words properly.

   Write the following words on the board: **letter, ladder, mommy, middle.**

   Ask the students to arrange these words in ABC order: **ladder, letter, middle,**

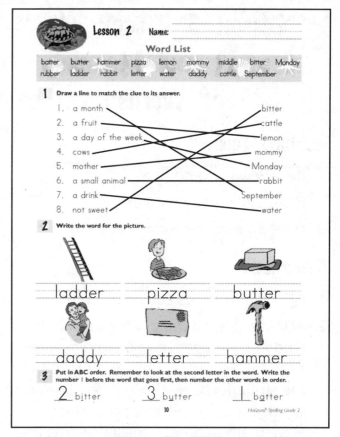

mommy. Point out that they needed to go to the second letter of the two "**l**" words to find the correct order and the second letter of the two "**m**" words.

Have the students look at the three words in Activity 3. Ask them to put these words in ABC order by numbering them **1, 2, 3.** Check for difficulties.

Extended Activities:

1. Give additional practice in ABC order using second and third letter clues. For third letter clues, you may begin with those in the spelling words: **lemon, letter, mommy, Monday.** Find additional examples. Words may be written on sets of cards and placed in the language arts learning center for additional practice.

2. Have the students continue the writing of sentences for each spelling word in their notebooks.

Lesson 3 - Look at Context and Meaning of Words

Teaching Tips:

1. Review words and rules.
2. Have Bible ready for story.
3. Have Spelling dictionaries available.

Activities:

1. Give the students Lesson 3.

2. **Activity 1:** Read the directions with the students. If pages have been removed from the Spelling books, make sure that the students have a copy of the Spelling words for the week in front of them. Have them circle ALL spelling words that they find in the story, even if they are repeated.

3. **Activity 2:** Ask the students to write the spelling words they have found on the lines provided. EACH WORD WILL BE WRITTEN ONLY ONCE.

4. **Activity 3:** Read the Bible story to the students. Ask them which spelling word(s) they heard in the story (**water**). Ask them to draw a picture to go with the story. Have them write a sentence using the word "**water**" as it is used in the story.

Extended Activities:

1. Ask about other Bible stories in which water plays a part: Noah, Moses as a baby, crossing of the Red Sea, Baptism of Jesus, etc.

2. Make a bulletin board of picture stories from the Bible in which water plays a major role.

3. Have the students continue the writing of sentences for each spelling word in their notebooks.

Lesson 4 - Apply Understanding of Words in Writing

Teaching Tips:

1. Have Spelling dictionaries available.
2. Have paper available for sentence activity.

Activities:

1. Give the students Lesson 4.
2. **Writing Activity 1:** Read the directions with the students. Make sure that they each have paper. Brainstorm a few sentences with the students and write them on the board. Ask the students to write their own sentences on their paper.
3. **Writing Activity 2:** Ask the students if they have ever helped to make a pizza. Imagine what it would be like. What would each member of the family do to help? What toppings would each want? Ask the students to write a story about what it would be like if their family decided to make their own pizza instead of going out for it or having it delivered. Give help as needed.

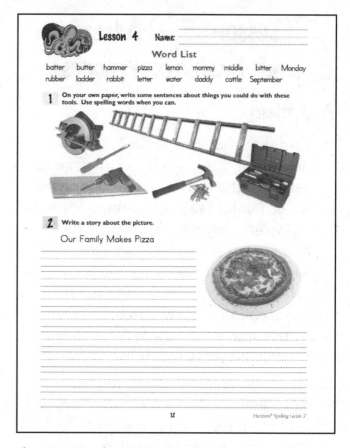

Extended Activities:

1. Share stories.
2. Have the students continue the writing of sentences for each spelling word in their notebooks.

Lesson 5 - Assess and Evaluate Progress

Activities:

1. Give the students Lesson 5. Tell the students that this is a "Check-up" page to see what they have learned during the week. [**Note:** Teachers/parents of home schoolers may decide what will be assessed. If a student does exceptionally well on the "What do you know?" pre-assessment, the teacher may choose not to test words already known by the student. Or the teacher may choose to test all words for the week.]

2. Tell the students that you will say a word and use it in a sentence. They will listen to the word and the sentence. Then, they will write the word on the line next to the numbers. All working words are included in this review.

3. Say the word. Repeat it in the context of a sentence. Repeat the word.

4. The students write the word dictated.

5. The process is repeated until all words have been tested.

6. The teacher may correct in class by writing the words on the board and having the students compare or "self-correct" their work. Or the teacher may correct each student's work individually.

7. The teacher then writes any corrections for words misspelled in the space provided.

8. The students study the misspelled words, then practice them on the second side of the Lesson page.

9. Space is provided for retesting, for testing additional sight or "working words" added for the week, and for additional practice.

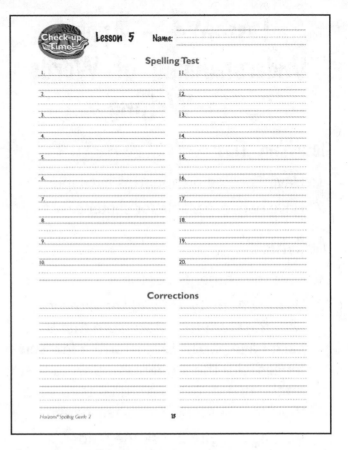

Extended Activity:

Review any words missed. Send words to review home for additional study. Praise all efforts.

Week 2

Lessons 6-10 - Assess Student's Knowledge

Goal: To learn to recognize and spell words with the short ă, ĭ, and ŭ sounds.

Short Vowel Symbol: Review the short vowel sign (˘) with the students and have them practice writing it. This symbol is called a **breve**.

Short Vowel Rule: When a word or syllable has only one vowel and it comes between two consonants, or at the beginning of the word or syllable, the vowel is usually short. Examples: **ăt, măn, păn, pĭn, tĭn, fŭn, rŭn**.

Rule for Capital Letters: Names of people, months, days of the week, and special places begin with a capital letter.

What Do You Know?

Give the students the What do you know? page for Lessons 6–10. Tell them that this page will be used to see what they already know about the words for the week. Ask them to listen carefully to each word as you say it, repeat it in a sentence, and say it once again. Follow the procedures for this page as described in the *Introduction* at the beginning of this Teacher's Guide.

Show the children how to write their working words in the appropriate section at the back of their *Spelling Dictionary*.

Words for the Week   **Corrections**   **Practice**

1. math
2. sat
3. tan
4. map
5. path
6. winter
7. tip
8. win
9. sip
10. lip
11. summer
12. tug
13. tub
14. such
15. scrub
16. August
17. Sunday

Horizons Spelling Grade 2   15

Weeks 2 & 3: Short Vowel Rule

When a word or syllable has only one vowel, and it comes between two consonants or at the beginning of a word or syllable, the vowel is usually *short*.

Examples: ăt, măn, pĕt, pĭn, fŭn.

The symbol for the short vowel sound is called a *breve* (˘).

156   *Horizons® Spelling Grade 2*

Lesson 6 - Introduce Words

Activities:

1. Give the students Lesson 6.

2. Review the sounds of short ă, ĭ, and ŭ.

3. **Activity 1:** Ask the students to write the missing vowels on the spaces provided in each word. Check.

4. **Activity 2:** Ask the students to find all the spelling words that have the short ŭ sound and write them on the lines provided.

5. **Activity 3:** Ask the students to find all the spelling words that have the short ĭ sound and write them on the lines provided.

6. **Activity 4:** Write the working words chosen for the week on the board. Ask the students to write all five of their working words for the week on the lines provided.

7. **Activity 5:** Students will write their working words in their Spelling dictionaries in the back section. Words are to be written under the correct letter of the alphabet.

8. Remember that all pages should be removed from the Student Workbook to promote good penmanship.

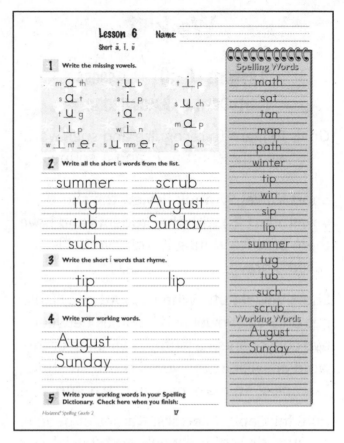

Extended Activities for the Week:

1. Send a list of the week's words home for further study. Emphasize the importance of using spelling words in sentences, in speech, in stories, etc., so that they are given a context and not simply memorized in isolation.

2. Assign reproducible *Week 2 Worksheet* either as homework or as an added classroom activity.

3. Have students write the definitions of the "choice" working words in their notebooks.

4. Have the students begin the writing of sentences for each spelling word in their notebooks.

5. Bring out or begin word family charts for short vowel words.

Lesson 7 - Examine and Explore Words

Activities:

1. Give the students Lesson 7.

2. Review word shapes with the students. Write the spelling words for the week on the board. Draw shapes around two or three of the words. Ask students to come to the board and draw shapes around the remaining words. Then erase the words and draw the shapes for the words: **Sunday**, **tub**, **sip**, and **winter**. Ask the students to look at their spelling lists and find a word that will fit the shape. Have individual students come to the board and write in the letters. [**Note:** the word **map** has the same shape as **sip**. Accept either word.]

3. **Activity 1:** Review the pictures with the students. Ask them to find the shape of the word which describes each picture. Have them write the word in the shape, and then, draw a line from the picture to the word.

4. **Activities 2 & 3:** These activities review the rule for capitalization of months and days of the year. Have the students find first the name of a month and write it in a sentence. Have them find the name for the day of the week and write it in a sentence. Share sentences and check.

5. **Activity 4:** This activity reviews syllables. Have the students say each of their spelling words and ask them to clap for each syllable they hear in a word. Have them write the words with two syllables on the lines provided.

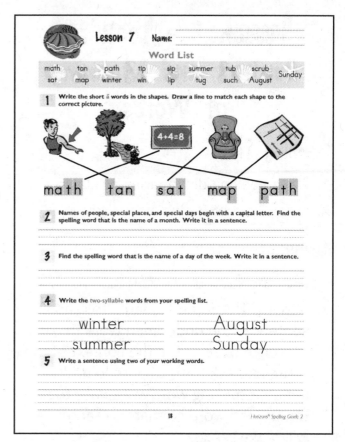

6. Review the five working words for the week. Ask the students to use two of them in a sentence. USE THE WORKING WORDS OF CHOICE FOR THIS ACTIVITY, not the two given as part of the word list.

Extended Activities:

1. Provide additional practice as needed on word shapes, capitals and syllable practice.

2. Have the students continue the writing of sentences for each spelling word in their notebooks.

Lesson 8 – Look at Context and Meaning of Words

Teaching Tips:

1. Have Spelling dictionaries available.
2. Have Bible or Bible verse ready.

Activities:

1. Give the students Lesson 8.
2. **Activity 1:** Ask the students to read each sentence. The underlined word in each sentence does not fit the context of the sentence. Ask the students to find a suitable spelling word to replace the underlined word so that the sentence will make sense.
3. **Activity 2:** Have the students complete the word puzzles by adding or subtracting the letters as indicated. Write the new words on the lines provided.
4. **Activity 3:** Read the Bible verse with the students. Discuss the seasons of the year as they occur in the area. Have the students write a letter to God thanking him for the seasons.

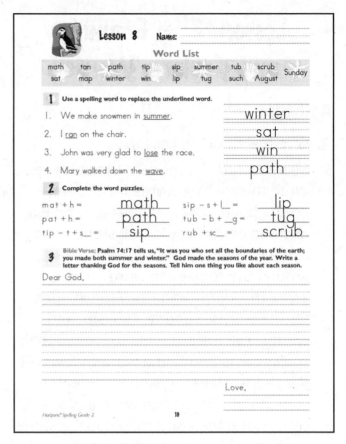

Extended Activities:

1. Have the students continue the writing of sentences for each spelling word in their notebooks.
2. If students had difficulty with Activity 2, provide additional practice. Word puzzles, such as the ones given, can be made on flash cards and placed in the learning center to give students additional practice.

Lesson 9 - Apply Understanding of Words in Writing

Teaching Tips:

1. Have Spelling dictionaries available.
2. Have some simple sample maps on hand to aid students in Activity 2.

Activities:

1. Give the students Lesson 9.
2. **Writing Activity 1:** Discuss the two pictures with the students noting details in each. Ask the students to write about one of the pictures using as many spelling words as they can. Encourage them to use their Spelling dictionaries as needed. Check.
3. **Mapping Activity 2:** Demonstrate this activity on the board for the students. Choose something familiar to all of them: the classroom or school campus; the neighborhood, etc. After the demonstration map is completed, ask the students create their own maps of a different place.

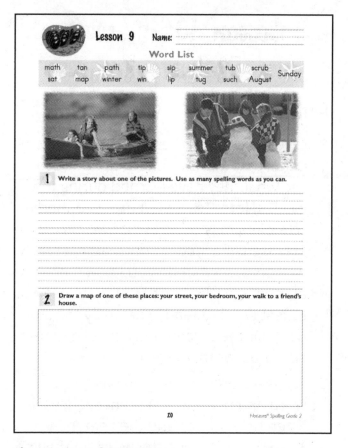

Extended Activities:

1. Share stories.
2. Share maps.
3. Have the students continue the writing of sentences for each spelling word in their notebooks.

Lesson 10 - Assess and Evaluate Progress

Activities:

1. Give the students Lesson 10. Tell the students that this is a "Check-up" page to see what they have learned during the week. [**Note:** Teachers/parents of home schoolers may decide what will be assessed. If a student does exceptionally well on the "What do you know?" pre-assessment, the teacher may choose not to test words already known by the student. Or the teacher may choose to test all words for the week.]

2. Tell the students that you will say a word and use it in a sentence. They will listen to the word and the sentence. Then they will write the word on the line next to the numbers. All working words are included in this review.

3. Say the word. Repeat it in the context of a sentence. Repeat the word.

4. The students write the word dictated.

5. The process is repeated until all words have been tested.

6. The teacher may correct in class by writing the words on the board and having the students compare or "self-correct" their work. Or the teacher may correct each student's work individually.

7. The teacher then writes any corrections for words misspelled in the space provided.

8. The students study the misspelled words, then practice them on the second side of the Lesson page.

9. Space is provided for retesting, for testing additional sight or "working words" added for the week, and for additional practice.

Check-up Time! Lesson 10 Name: _____

Spelling Test

1.	11.
2.	12.
3.	13.
4.	14.
5.	15.
6.	16.
7.	17.
8.	18.
9.	19.
10.	20.

Corrections

Horizons® Spelling Grade 2　　21

Extended Activity:

Review any words missed. Send words to review home for additional study. Praise all efforts.

Week 3

Lessons 11-15 - Assess Student's Knowledge

Goal: To recognize and spell words with short ŏ and ĕ sounds.

Review Short Vowel Rule: When a word or syllable has only one vowel and it comes between two consonants, or at the beginning of the word or syllable, the vowel is usually short. Examples: **hŏt**, **gŏt**, **mĕn**, **gĕt**.

What Do You Know?

Give the students the What do you know? page for Lessons 11-15. Tell them that this page will be used to see what they already know about the words for the week. Ask them to listen carefully to each word as you say it, repeat it in a sentence, and say it once again. Follow the procedures for this page as described in the *Introduction* at the beginning of this Teacher's Guide.

Show the children how to write their working words in the appropriate section at the back of their *Spelling Dictionary*.

What do you know?

Lessons 11-15 Name: _____

Words for the Week	Corrections	Practice
1. sock	1.	1.
2. hot	2.	2.
3. pond	3.	3.
4. nod	4.	4.
5. top	5.	5.
6. cob	6.	6.
7. mop	7.	7.
8. met	8.	8.
9. pencil	9.	9.
10. men	10.	10.
11. leg	11.	11.
12. belt	12.	12.
13. pet	13.	13.
14. stem	14.	14.
15. hem	15.	15.
16. second	16.	16.
17. off	17.	17.

Horizons Spelling Grade 2　　　　25

Weeks 2 & 3: Short Vowel Rule

When a word or syllable has only one vowel, and it comes between two consonants or at the beginning of a word or syllable, the vowel is usually *short*.

Examples: ăt, măn, pĕt, pĭn, fŭn.

The symbol for the short vowel sound is called a *breve* (˘).

256　　　　*Horizons® Spelling Grade 2*

Lesson 11 - Introduce Words

Teaching Tip:

Have Spelling dictionaries available.

Activities:

1. Give the students Lesson 11.

2. Review sounds of short **ŏ** and **ĕ**.

3. **Activity 1:** Ask the students to draw a line from the picture to the spelling word.

4. **Activity 2:** Ask the students to find and write the short **ĕ** spelling words ending with the consonant **m**.

5. **Activity 3:** Ask the students to find and write the short **ĕ** spelling words ending with the consonant **t**.

6. **Activity 4:** Have the students fill in the missing vowels for the three spelling words given.

7. **Activity 5:** Write the working words chosen for the week on the board. Ask the students to write all five of their working words for the week on the lines provided.

8. **Activity 6:** Students will write their working words in their Spelling dictionaries in the back section. Words are to be written under the correct letter of the alphabet.

9. Remember that all pages should be removed from the Student Workbook to promote good penmanship.

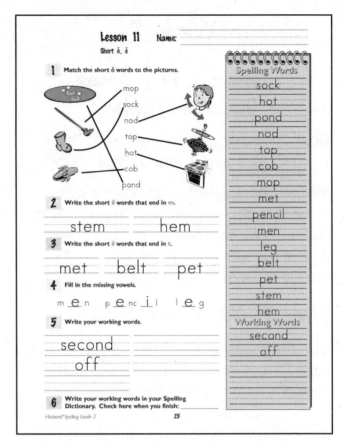

Extended Activities for the Week:

1. Send a list of the week's words home for further study. Emphasize the importance of using spelling words in sentences, in speech, in stories, etc., so that they are given a context and not simply memorized in isolation.

2. Assign reproducible *Week 3 Worksheet* either as homework or as an added classroom activity.

3. Have students write the definitions of the "choice" working words in their notebooks.

4. Have the students begin the writing of sentences for each spelling word in their notebooks.

5. Continue word family charts for short vowel words.

Lesson 12 - Examine and Explore Words

Activities:

1. Give the students Lesson 12.

2. **Activity 1:** Review syllables. Ask the students to circle the two-syllable words in the spelling list.

3. **Activity 2:** Ask the students to look at the words given in the activity. Ask them how the vowel in each word can be changed to make a spelling word. Have them write the spelling word on the line next to the word.

4. **Activity 3:** Tell the students that each set of words is a riddle. The students are to find a spelling word that will solve the riddle and write it on the line next to the clues.

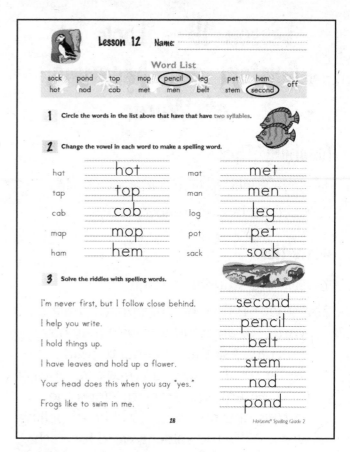

Extended Activities:

1. If students have difficulty with the second activity, provide additional practice.

2. Have the students continue the writing of sentences for each spelling word in their notebooks.

Lesson 13 - Look at Context and Meaning of Words

Teaching Tips:

1. Have Spelling dictionaries available.
2. Have Bible story ready.

Activities:

1. Give the students Lesson 13.

2. **Activity 1:** Give practice unscrambling words for any students who may have difficulty. Ask the students to read the sentences. In each sentence one word (underlined) is scrambled. When the word is unscrambled, it will be a spelling word. Write the spelling word for each sentence on the line provided.

3. **Activity 2:** Read the Bible story to the students. Discuss it with them. Who were the two men? How did each come before God? How did each pray? Ask the students to write a sentence about each man's prayer. Draw a picture to go with the sentences.

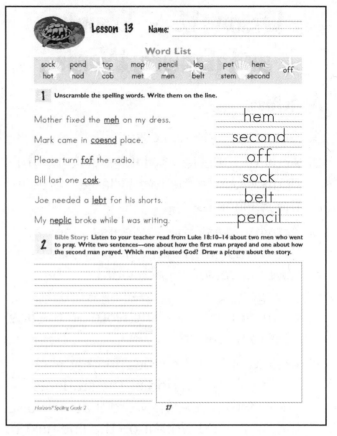

Extended Activities:

1. For students with visual discrimination problems, have pairs of word cards available in the learning center: one with a spelling word; one with the word scrambled. The students can make a game of matching the pairs. Try to keep the words short for now (3-5 letters).

2. Give students with difficulties individual letter cards or "scrabble" tiles to help them spell out the scrambled words.

3. Share Bible story summaries and pictures. Act out the Bible story as time allows.

4. Have the students continue the writing of sentences for each spelling word in their notebooks.

Lesson 14 - Apply Understanding of Words in Writing

Teaching Tip:

Have Spelling dictionaries available.

Activities:

1. Give the students Lesson 14.

2. **Writing Activity:** Discuss the picture with the students. Many "silly" things are pictured there. Ask the students to write a story from the girl's point of view. What does she see? What does she think about this "adventure" she has walked into?   Help as needed. Check.

Extended Activity:

Share stories with the class.

Lesson 15 - Assess and Evaluate Progress

Activities:

1. Give the students Lesson15. Tell the students that this is a "Check-up" page to see what they have learned during the week. [**Note:** Teachers/parents of home schoolers may decide what will be assessed. If a student does exceptionally well on the "What do you know?" pre-assessment, the teacher may choose not to test words already known by the student. Or the teacher may choose to test all words for the week.]

2. Tell the students that you will say a word and use it in a sentence. They will listen to the word and the sentence. Then they will write the word on the line next to the numbers. All working words are included in this review.

3. Say the word. Repeat it in the context of a sentence. Repeat the word.

4. The students write the word dictated.

5. The process is repeated until all words have been tested.

6. The teacher may correct in class by writing the words on the board and having the students compare or "self-correct" their work. Or the teacher may correct each student's work individually.

7. The teacher then writes any corrections for words misspelled in the space provided.

8. The students study the misspelled words, then practice them on the second side of the Lesson page.

9. Space is provided for retesting, for testing additional sight or "working words" added for the week, and for additional practice.

Check-up Time! Lesson 15   Name:

Spelling Test

1.	11.
2.	12.
3.	13.
4.	14.
5.	15.
6.	16.
7.	17.
8.	18.
9.	19.
10.	20.

Corrections

Horizons Spelling Grade 2   29

Extended Activity:

Review any words missed. Send words to review home for additional study. Praise all efforts.

Week 4

Lessons 16-20 - Assess Student's Knowledge

Goal: To recognize and spell words with long $\bar{a}$, $\bar{i}$, and $\bar{u}$ sounds.

Long Vowel Symbol: Review the long vowel sign (¯) with the students and have them practice writing it. This symbol is called a **macron**.

Long Vowel Rule: When a word or syllable has two vowels, the first vowel is usually long and the second vowel is usually silent: **name, pain, pay, smile, bind, huge, true.**

What Do You Know?

Give the students the What do you know? page for Lessons 16-20. Tell them that this page will be used to see what they already know about the words for the week. Ask them to listen carefully to each word as you say it, repeat it in a sentence, and say it once again. Follow the procedures for this page as described in the *Introduction* at the beginning of this Teacher's Guide.

Show the children how to write their working words in the appropriate section at the back of their *Spelling Dictionary*.

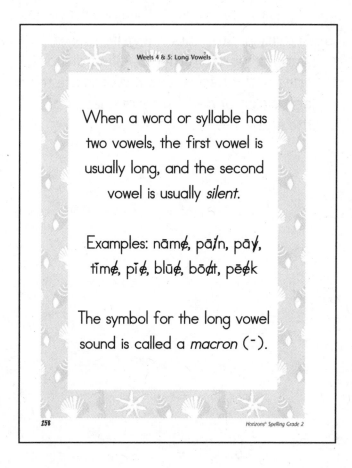

What do you know? Lessons 16-20 Name: _____

Words for the Week	Corrections	Practice
1. United		1.
2. States		2.
3. day		3.
4. clay		4.
5. wait		5.
6. trail		6.
7. bind		7.
8. sight		8.
9. pine		9.
10. tile		10.
11. smile		11.
12. huge		12.
13. flew		13.
14. true		14.
15. new		15.
16. Saturday		16.
17. July		17.

Horizons Spelling Grade 2   31

Weeks 4 & 5: Long Vowels

When a word or syllable has two vowels, the first vowel is usually long, and the second vowel is usually *silent*.

Examples: nāmé, pā/n, pāý, tīmé, pīé, blūé, bōǿt, pēǿk

The symbol for the long vowel sound is called a *macron* (˘).

258   *Horizons® Spelling Grade 2*

Lesson 16 - Introduce Words

Activities:

1. Give the students Lesson 16.

2. **Activity 1:** Review the different spellings for the long $\bar{a}$ sound. Ask the students to find and write the spelling words for each long $\bar{a}$ grouping given.

3. **Activity 2:** Review the different spellings for the long $\bar{i}$ sound. Ask the students to find and write the spelling words for each long $\bar{i}$ grouping given.

4. **Activity 3:** Have the students find and write the spelling word that has two long vowels: **i** and **u**.

5. **Activity 4:** Write the working words chosen for the week on the board. Ask the students to write all five of their working words for the week on the lines provided.

6. **Activity 5:** Students will write their working words in their Spelling dictionaries in the back section. Words are to be written under the correct letter of the alphabet.

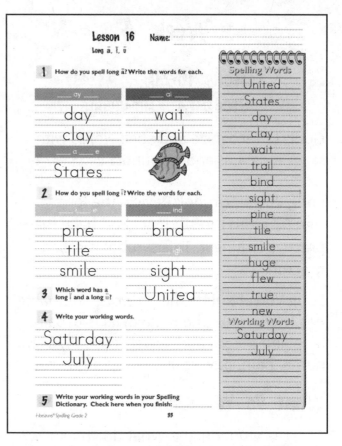

Extended Activities for the Week:

1. Send a list of the week's words home for further study. Emphasize the importance of using spelling words in sentences, in speech, in stories, etc., so that they are given a context and not simply memorized in isolation.

2. Assign reproducible *Week 4 Worksheet* either as homework or as an added classroom activity.

3. Have students write the definitions of the "choice" working words in their notebooks.

4. Have the students begin the writing of sentences for each spelling word in their notebooks.

5. Bring out or begin word family charts for long vowel words and patterns for each long vowel.

Lesson 17 - Examine and Explore Words

Activities:

1. Give the students Lesson 17.

2. **Activity 1:** Crossword Puzzle. Review crossword puzzles. Read through the first few clues with the students. Check to make sure they are entering the words in the correct boxes. Allow the students to complete independently as they are able.

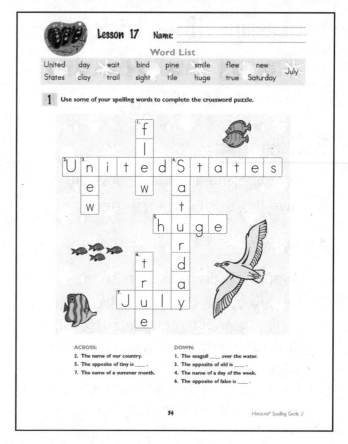

Extended Activities:

1. Add any new words for the long vowel patterns to the individual long vowel family chart:

   Long $\bar{a}$: a__e, ai, ay,
   Long $\bar{i}$: i__e, -ind, igh,
   Long $\bar{u}$: u__e, ew, ue.

2. Have the students continue the writing of sentences for each spelling word in their notebooks.

Lesson 18 - Look at Context and Meaning of Words

Teaching Tips:

1. Have Spelling dictionaries available.
2. Have Bible or Bible verse ready.

Activities:

1. Give the students Lesson 18.

2. **Activity 1:** The students will use ten spelling words to complete this story (**Saturday**, **July**, **trail**, **day**, **clay**, **pine**, **huge**, **flew**, **sight**, **smile**). Have the students read the sentences aloud, decide which spelling words will complete them, and write the spelling words in the correct space.

3. **Activity 2:** Review the five working words for the week. Ask the students to use two of them in a sentence. USE THE WORKING WORDS OF CHOICE FOR THIS ACTIVITY, not the two given as part of the word list.

4. **Activity 3:** Read the Bible verse with the students. Perhaps it could be used as a prayer throughout the day. Ask the students to write the verse on the lines provided, to learn the verse by heart, and to share it with a friend.

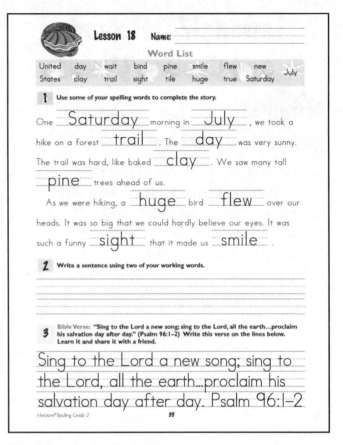

Extended Activities:

1. Have materials available in the learning center for the students to write their own stories to go with this week's words.

2. Have the students continue the writing of sentences for each spelling word in their notebooks. [**Note:** The two words used in Activity 2 do NOT need to be done in the notebook this week.]

Lesson 19 - Apply Understanding of Words in Writing

Teaching Tip:

Have Spelling dictionaries available.

Activities:

1. Give the students Lesson 19.
2. **Writing Activity:** Use the directions as a "brainstorming" activity for the story to be written. What would they do? Would they go on a picnic? Would they see a movie? Would they take a day at the park? How about a day at the beach? [**Note:** For our students south of the equator, write what you might do on a "Winter" day in July!]
3. Help as needed. Check.

Lesson 19 Name: _____

Word List

| United States | day | wait | bind | pine | smile | flew | new | July |
| | clay | trail | sight | tile | huge | true | Saturday | |

1 Think back to a summer Saturday. What do you remember? What things did you do? Draw a picture and use as many of your spelling words as you can to write a story.

A Summer Saturday in July

36

Horizons Spelling Grade 2

Extended Activities:

1. Share stories, pictures and experiences.
2. Have the students continue the writing of sentences for each spelling word in their notebooks.

Lesson 20 - Assess and Evaluate Progress

Activities:

1. Give the students Lesson 20. Tell the students that this is a "Check-up" page to see what they have learned during the week. [**Note:** Teachers/parents of home schoolers may decide what will be assessed. If a student does exceptionally well on the "What do you know?" pre-assessment, the teacher may choose not to test words already known by the student. Or the teacher may choose to test all words for the week.]

2. Tell the students that you will say a word and use it in a sentence. They will listen to the word and the sentence. Then they will write the word on the line next to the numbers. All working words are included in this review.

3. Say the word. Repeat it in the context of a sentence. Repeat the word.

4. The students write the word dictated.

5. The process is repeated until all words have been tested.

6. The teacher may correct in class by writing the words on the board and having the students compare or "self-correct" their work. Or the teacher may correct each student's work individually.

7. The teacher then writes any corrections for words misspelled in the space provided.

8. The students study the misspelled words, then practice them on the second side of the Lesson page.

9. Space is provided for retesting, for testing additional sight or "working words" added for the week, and for additional practice.

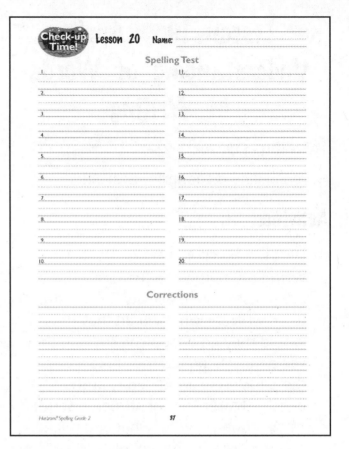

Extended Activity:

Review any words missed. Send words to review home for additional study. Praise all efforts.

Horizons Spelling Grade 2

Week 5

Lessons 21-25 - Assess Student's Knowledge

Goal: To recognize and spell words with the long ō and long ē sound.

Review Long Vowel Rules:

When a word or syllable has two vowels, the first vowel is usually long and the second vowel is usually silent: **boat**, **roam**, **broke**, **peek**, **neat**.

When a word or syllable has just one vowel, and the vowel comes at the end of the word or syllable, the vowel sound is usually long: **be**, **go**, **Tony**.

What Do You Know?

Give the students the What do you know? page for Lessons 21-25. Tell them that this page will be used to see what they already know about the words for the week. Ask them to listen carefully to each word as you say it, repeat it in a sentence, and say it once again. Follow the procedures for this page as described in the *Introduction* at the beginning of this Teacher's Guide.

Show the children how to write their working words in the appropriate section at the back of their *Spelling Dictionary*.

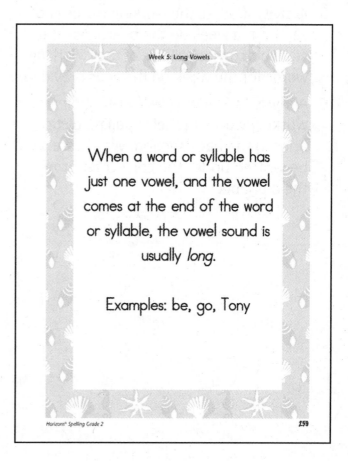

Lesson 21 - Introduce Words

Activities:

1. Give the students Lesson 21.

2. **Activity 1:** Review the different spellings for the long ō sound. Ask the students to find and write the spelling words for each long ō grouping given.

3. **Activity 2:** Ask the students to add the vowel needed to complete the two spelling words given. (Check the spelling of **believe**.)

4. **Activity 3:** Review the different spellings for the long ē sound. Ask the students to look at the shapes given. Ask them to find the long ē spelling words that fit into the shapes. Write the words in the shapes and circle the long ē groupings.

5. **Activity 4:** Write the working words chosen for the week on the board. Ask the students to write all five of their working words for the week on the lines provided.

6. **Activity 5:** Students will write their working words in their Spelling dictionaries in the back section. Words are to be written under the correct letter of the alphabet.

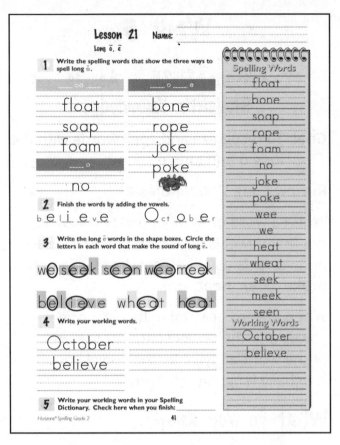

Extended Activities for the Week:

1. Send a list of the week's words home for further study. Emphasize the importance of using spelling words in sentences, in speech, in stories, etc., so that they are given a context and not simply memorized in isolation.

2. Assign reproducible *Week 5 Worksheet* either as homework or as an added classroom activity.

3. Have students write the definitions of the "choice" working words in their notebooks.

4. Have the students begin the writing of sentences for each spelling word in their notebooks.

5. Bring out or begin word family charts for long ō and long ē vowel words.

Lesson 22 - Examine and Explore Words

Activities:

1. Give the students Lesson 22.

2. **Activity 1:** Each sentence in this activity contains 1 misspelled word that stands for and sounds like a spelling word from the list. Ask the students to find the misspelled word, circle it, then write the correct spelling word on the line provided.

3. **Activity 2:** This is a dictionary activity. Ask the students to take their Spelling dictionaries and look up the words "poke" and "joke." Ask them to write the definition on the line provided. Assist students who may still have difficulty finding words in the dictionary.

4. **Activity 3:** Have students find and write the two-syllable spelling word.

5. **Activity 4:** The name of the month, October, has three syllables. Have the students write the word in syllables. Encourage them to use their dictionaries if they are unsure of the division.

6. **Activity 5:** This activity gives additional dictionary practice. Have the students arrange the words in ABC order. Give review or added practice for students who continue to have difficulty in this area.

Extended Activities:

1. Have additional sets of this week's words available in the learning center for ABC order practice. Have students work together if some are having difficulties.

2. Give additional words for students to find in their dictionaries if further practice is needed.

3. Have the students continue the writing of sentences for each spelling word in their notebooks.

Lesson 23 - Look at Context and Meaning of Words

Teaching Tips:

1. Have Spelling dictionaries available.
2. Have Bible or Bible verse ready.

Activities:

1. Give the students Lesson 23.
2. **Activity 1:** Write the first three words: **soap, float, foam,** on the board. Ask the students for ideas for a sentence that would use all three words. Write their ideas on the board. Have the students write their own sentences and draw a picture to go with the sentence. Allow them to do the second sentence independently.
3. **Activity 2:** Read the Bible verses to the students and talk about what they mean. Have the students write a prayer to Jesus asking his help.

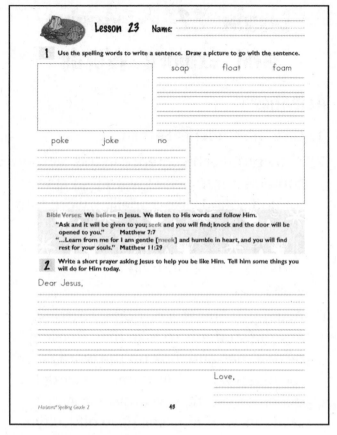

Extended Activities:

1. Have additional word groupings from this lesson available in the learning center for further sentence practice. (Examples: **seek, meek, believe; bone, rope, wee; heat, wheat, October,** etc.)
2. Have the students continue the writing of sentences for each spelling word in their notebooks.

Lesson 24 - Apply Understanding of Words in Writing

Teaching Tips:

1. Have Spelling dictionaries available.
2. Have additional pictures of October activities available, especially any that are specific to your area.

Activities:

1. Give the students Lesson 24.
2. **Writing Activity:** Talk about the month of October with the students. What holidays are in October? Are there any other special days? Does anyone have a birthday? What kind of weather do they see in October? Discuss the pictures given and compare them with the students' experiences.
3. Have the students write their own October story telling things that they like to do.

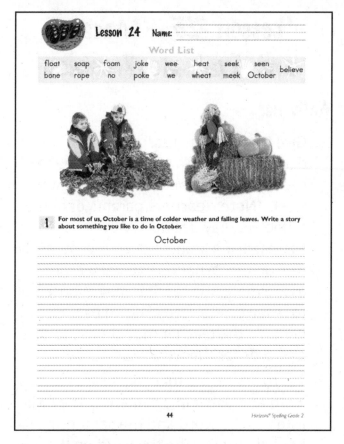

Extended Activities:

1. Share student stories with class.
2. Make an "October collage."
3. Have the students continue the writing of sentences for each spelling word in their notebooks.

Lesson 25 - Assess and Evaluate Progress

Activities:

1. Give the students Lesson 25. Tell the students that this is a "Check-up" page to see what they have learned during the week. [**Note:** Teachers/parents of home schoolers may decide what will be assessed. If a student does exceptionally well on the "What do you know?" pre-assessment, the teacher may choose not to test words already known by the student. Or the teacher may choose to test all words for the week.]

2. Tell the students that you will say a word and use it in a sentence. They will listen to the word and the sentence. Then they will write the word on the line next to the numbers. All working words are included in this review.

3. Say the word. Repeat it in the context of a sentence. Repeat the word.

4. The students write the word dictated.

5. The process is repeated until all words have been tested.

6. The teacher may correct in class by writing the words on the board and having the students compare or "self-correct" their work. Or the teacher may correct each student's work individually.

7. The teacher then writes any corrections for words misspelled in the space provided.

8. The students study the misspelled words, then practice them on the second side of the Lesson page.

9. Space is provided for retesting, for testing additional sight or "working words" added for the week, and for additional practice.

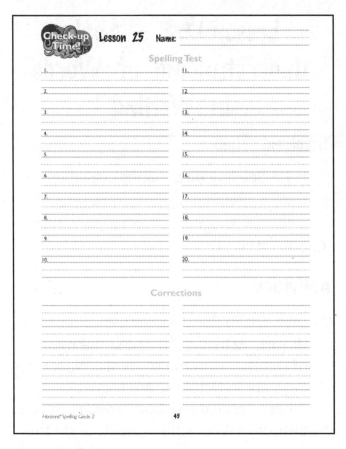

Extended Activity:

Review any words missed. Send words to review home for additional study. Praise all efforts.

Week 6

Lessons 26-30 - Assess Student's Knowledge

Goal: To recognize and spell compound words.

Review Rule: A compound word is a word made from two or more words joined together to make one word. Ex.: **backyard**, **runway**, **mailbox**.

What Do You Know?

Give the students the What do you know? page for Lessons 26-30. Tell them that this page will be used to see what they already know about the words for the week. Ask them to listen carefully to each word as you say it, repeat it in a sentence, and say it once again. Follow the procedures for this page as described in the *Introduction* at the beginning of this Teacher's Guide.

Show the children how to write their working words in the appropriate section at the back of their *Spelling Dictionary*.

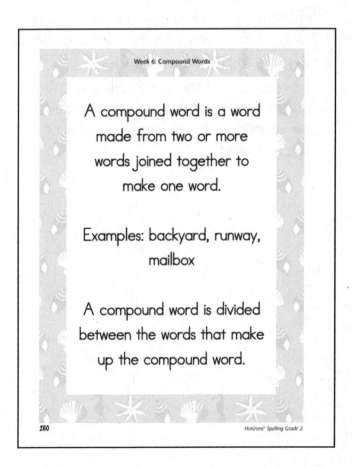

What do you know? Lessons 26-30	Name:	
Words for the Week	**Corrections**	**Practice**
1 baseball		
2 nowhere		
3 airplane		
4 anyone		
5 someone		
6 forgot		
7 friendship		
8 foxhole		
9 headache		
10 tightrope		
11 somehow		
12 meatloaf		
13 moonlight		
14 patchwork		
15 bedroom		
16 Tuesday		
17 fourth		

Horizons Spelling Grade 2   47

Week 6: Compound Words

A compound word is a word made from two or more words joined together to make one word.

Examples: backyard, runway, mailbox

A compound word is divided between the words that make up the compound word.

160   *Horizons® Spelling Grade 2*

Lesson 26 - Introduce Words

Activities:

1. Give the students Lesson 26.

2. Ask the students for examples of compound words. Write the students' suggestions on the board.

3. **Activity 1:** Have the students match the words in the first column to the partner in the second column needed to make one of the spelling words.

4. **Activity 2:** Ask the students to say the names of the pictures that make up a compound word. Have the students find the word in their spelling list and write it on the line provided.

5. **Activity 3:** Write the working words chosen for the week on the board. Ask the students to write all five of their working words for the week on the lines provided.

6. **Activity 4:** Students will write their working words in their Spelling dictionaries in the back section. Words are to be written under the correct letter of the alphabet.

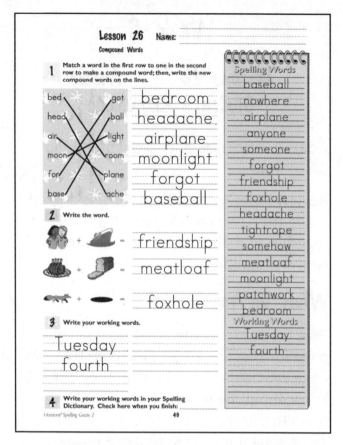

Extended Activities for the Week:

1. Send a list of the week's words home for further study. Emphasize the importance of using spelling words in sentences, in speech, in stories, etc., so that they are given a context and not simply memorized in isolation.

2. Assign reproducible *Week 6 Worksheet* either as homework or as an added classroom activity.

3. Have students write the definitions of the "choice" working words in their notebooks.

4. Have the students begin the writing of sentences for each spelling word in their notebooks.

5. Bring out or begin word family charts for compound words. [**Note:** compound words may also belong to one of the short or long vowel families. Point out patterns.]

Lesson 27 – Examine and Explore Words

Activities:

1. Give the students Lesson 27.

2. **Activity 1:** This activity gives more practice in combining words to make compound words. This time the compound word is given at the end of the line. The students need to recognize the two words that make up the compound. One half of the word is given. The students need to write the missing half of the compound on the line provided.

3. **Activity 2:** The students will finish the sentences using words from the spelling list. The first letter of each word is provided.

Extended Activities:

1. Have two sets of word cards in the learning center for this week's words: one set of the complete words and one set of the individual words that make up the compound words for the week. Have students match and make new words if possible.

2. Have the students continue the writing of sentences for each spelling word in their notebooks.

Lesson 28 - Look at Context and Meaning of Words

Teaching Tips:

1. Have Spelling dictionaries available.
2. Have Bible ready for story.

Activities:

1. Give the students Lesson 28.
2. **Activity 1:** The ten spelling words given in the word box are hidden in the sentences of this activity. Have the students read the first sentence. What two words in that sentence, when put together, will make one of the compound spelling words in the box? Have the students circle the two words in the sentence and write the compound word on the line provided.
3. **Activity 2:** Read the Bible Story to the students. Talk about Jesus' love for each of us. Ask the students how they can be like Jesus, how they can be his friend and a true friend to others. Have them write their reflections on the lines provided.

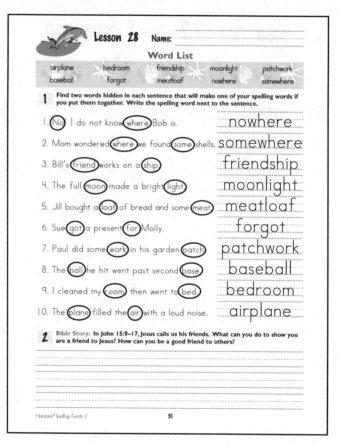

Extended Activities:

1. Share reflections. Talk about other places in the Bible where Jesus talks about ways to show our love for him and for each other.
2. Have the students continue the writing of sentences for each spelling word in their notebooks.

Lesson 29 - Apply Understanding of Words in Writing

Teaching Tip:

Have Spelling dictionaries available.

Activities:

1. Give the students Lesson 29.
2. **Writing Activity:** Have the students discuss the picture. How many pictures for compound words do they see? Ask the students to write a story about the picture.
3. Have the students color the picture.

Extended Activities:

1. Share stories.
2. Have the students continue the writing of sentences for each spelling word in their notebooks.

Lesson 30 - Assess and Evaluate Progress

Activities:

1. Give the students Lesson 30. Tell the students that this is a "Check-up" page to see what they have learned during the week. [**Note:** Teachers/parents of home schoolers may decide what will be assessed. If a student does exceptionally well on the "What do you know?" pre-assessment, the teacher may choose not to test words already known by the student. Or the teacher may choose to test all words for the week.]

2. Tell the students that you will say a word and use it in a sentence. They will listen to the word and the sentence. Then they will write the word on the line next to the numbers. All working words are included in this review.

3. Say the word. Repeat it in the context of a sentence. Repeat the word.

4. The students write the word dictated.

5. The process is repeated until all words have been tested.

6. The teacher may correct in class by writing the words on the board and having the students compare or "self-correct" their work. Or the teacher may correct each student's work individually.

7. The teacher then writes any corrections for words misspelled in the space provided.

8. The students study the misspelled words, then practice them on the second side of the Lesson page.

9. Space is provided for retesting, for testing additional sight or "working words" added for the week, and for additional practice.

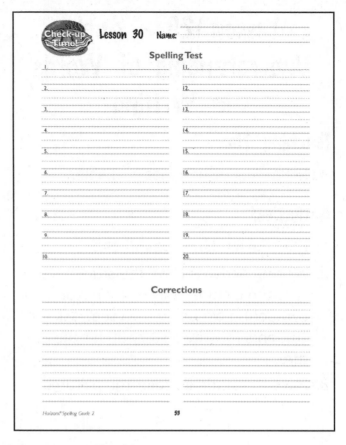

Extended Activity:

Review any words missed. Send words to review home for additional study. Praise all efforts.

Horizons Spelling Grade 2

Week 7

Lessons 31-35 - Assess Student's Knowledge

Goal: To recognize and spell words with **r** blends. To recognize and spell words using **y** as a consonant/vowel.

Review Rules:

In an **r** blend, two or more consonants come together in a word. Their sounds blend together, but each sound is heard. Examples: **green**, **frog**, **tree**.

Sometimes **y** can stand for the vowel sound of long $\bar{e}$ or long $\bar{i}$.

When y is the only vowel at the end of a one-syllable word, **y** usually has the long $\bar{i}$ sound. Examples: **my**, **by**.

When y is the only vowel at the end of a word of more than one syllable, **y** usually has the long $\bar{e}$ sound. Example: **baby**.

What Do You Know?

Give the students the What do you know? page for Lessons 31-35. Tell them that this page will be used to see what they already know about the words for the week. Ask them to listen carefully to each word as you say it, repeat it in a sentence, and say it once again. Follow the procedures for this page as described in the *Introduction* at the beginning of this Teacher's Guide.

Show the children how to write their working words in the appropriate section at the back of their *Spelling Dictionary*.

What do you know?
Lessons 31-35   Name: _____

Words for the Week   **Corrections**   **Practice**

1. fries
2. train
3. cross
4. praise
5. brave
6. dream
7. grade
8. throne
9. cry
10. trust
11. yak
12. yam
13. yell
14. baby
15. by
16. Wednesday
17. fifth

Horizons Spelling Grade 2   55

Week 7: R Blends

In an *r* blend, two or more consonants come together in a word. Their sounds blend together, but each sound is heard.

Examples: green, frog, tree

Horizons Spelling Grade 2   261

Lesson 31 - Introduce Words

Activities:

1. Give the students Lesson 31.

2. **Activity 1:** [Provide assistance for students who have visual discrimination problems.] Ask the students to look at each scrambled word carefully. Have them find the spelling word from the list that matches the scrambled word. [Allow students scrap paper so that they can try out different combinations with the scrambled letters to help them find the word.] Have the students write the spelling word on the line provided and circle the **r** blend.

3. **Activity 2:** Review words in which the **y** has the sound of long $\bar{i}$ (**my**, **why**, **fry**, **cry**, etc.). Ask the students to find and write the spelling word in which the **y** has the sound of long $\bar{i}$.

4. **Activity 3:** Review words in which the **y** has the sound of long $\bar{e}$ (**funny**, **silly**, **mommy**, **daddy**, etc.). Ask the students to find and write the spelling word in which the **y** has the sound of long $\bar{e}$.

5. **Activity 4:** Write the working words chosen for the week on the board. Ask the students to write all five of their working words for the week on the lines provided.

6. **Activity 5:** Students will write their working words in their Spelling dictionaries in the back section. Words are to be written under the correct letter of the alphabet.

Extended Activities for the Week:

1. Send a list of the week's words home for further study. Emphasize the importance of using spelling words in sentences, in speech, in stories, etc., so that they are given a context and not simply memorized in isolation.

2. For students with visual discrimination difficulties, provide individual letter tiles or cards to help them in the first activity.

3. Assign reproducible *Week 7 Worksheet* either as homework or as an added classroom activity.

4. Have students write the definitions of the "choice" working words in their notebooks.

5. Have the students begin the writing of sentences for each spelling word in their notebooks.

6. Bring out or begin word family charts for **r** blends and for the different sounds of **y**.

Horizons Spelling Grade 2

Lesson 32 - Examine and Explore Words

Teaching Tip:

Have a calendar or chart with the days of the week available.

Activities:

1. Give the students Lesson 32.

2. **Activity 1:** Review the rules for capital letters. Have the students write a sentence using the spelling word that is the name of a day of the week (**Wednesday**).

3. **Activity 2:** Review all the names of days of the week that the students have learned so far this year (**Sunday, Monday, Tuesday, Wednesday**). Ask the students to write the names on the lines provided. The first letter is given for each.

4. **Activity 3:** Review sorting words by ABC order. Review looking to the second and even the third letter to find the correct order. Give help as needed.

Extended Activities:

1. Give additional practice to those who are having difficulty remembering the spelling of the names of weekdays.

2. Give additional practice to those who need help sorting ABC order by the second and third letter of a word. Have cards available in the learning center.

3. Have the students continue the writing of sentences for each spelling word in their notebooks.

Lesson 33 - Look at Context and Meaning of Words

Teaching Tips:

1. Have Spelling dictionaries available.
2. Have a Bible available with the verses from the first activity marked.

Activities:

1. Give the students Lesson 33.
2. **Activity 1:** All the sentences in this activity are taken from the Bible. The words **"praise"** and **"trust"** will be used more than once. Encourage the students to use the verses throughout the day as short prayers.
3. **Activity 2:** Ask the students to select one of their favorite verses from Activity 1 and write it on the lines provided.

Lesson 33 Name: _____

Word List

| fries | cross | brave | grade | cry | yak | yell | by | fifth |
| train | praise | dream | throne | trust | yam | baby | Wednesday |

1 The Bible teaches us how to live. Use your spelling words to finish these Bible verses. Look them up in the Bible if you need to. You will use some words more than once.

1. " _Praise_ the Lord from the heavens...
   Praise him, sun and moon,
   Praise him, all you shining stars." Psalm 148: 1, 3

2. "May I never boast except in the _cross_
   of our Lord Jesus Christ." Galatians 6:14

3. "He (Jesus) will be great...The Lord God will give
   him the _throne_ of his father, David..." Luke 1:32

4. "An angel of the Lord appeared to Joseph in a
   dream ." Matthew 2:13

5. "To you, O Lord, I lift up my soul; in you I
   trust O my God." Psalm 25:1

6. "Hear my prayer, O Lord, listen to my
   cry for help..." Psalm 39:12

7. " _Trust_ in the Lord with all your heart
   and lean not on your own understanding." Proverbs 3:5

2 Write one of these verses here. _____

Horizons Spelling Grade 2   59

Extended Activities:

1. Ask the students to share their favorite verses. Ask them what other verses they know and would like to share.
2. Have the students continue the writing of sentences for each spelling word in their notebooks.

Horizons Spelling Grade 2

Lesson 34 - Apply Understanding of Words in Writing

Teaching Tip:

Have Spelling dictionaries available.

Activities:

1. Give the students Lesson 34.

2. **Writing Activity:** Discuss the picture about a very funny dream.

3. Have the students write a story about the dream using as many spelling words as possible.

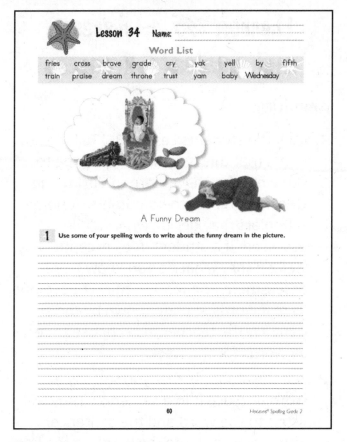

Extended Activities:

1. Share stories and experiences of funny dreams.

2. Have the students continue the writing of sentences for each spelling word in their notebooks.

Lesson 35 - Assess and Evaluate Progress

Activities:

1. Give the students Lesson 35. Tell the students that this is a "Check-up" page to see what they have learned during the week. [**Note:** Teachers/parents of home schoolers may decide what will be assessed. If a student does exceptionally well on the "What do you know?" pre-assessment, the teacher may choose not to test words already known by the student. Or the teacher may choose to test all words for the week.]

2. Tell the students that you will say a word and use it in a sentence. They will listen to the word and the sentence. Then they will write the word on the line next to the numbers. All working words are included in this review.

3. Say the word. Repeat it in the context of a sentence. Repeat the word.

4. The students write the word dictated.

5. The process is repeated until all words have been tested.

6. The teacher may correct in class by writing the words on the board and having the students compare or "self-correct" their work. Or the teacher may correct each student's work individually.

7. The teacher then writes any corrections for words misspelled in the space provided.

8. The students study the misspelled words, then practice them on the second side of the Lesson page.

9. Space is provided for retesting, for testing additional sight or "working words" added for the week, and for additional practice.

Check-up Time!   Lesson 35   Name: _____

Spelling Test

1. _____   11. _____
2. _____   12. _____
3. _____   13. _____
4. _____   14. _____
5. _____   15. _____
6. _____   16. _____
7. _____   17. _____
8. _____   18. _____
9. _____   19. _____
10. _____   20. _____

Corrections

Horizons Spelling Grade 2   61

Extended Activity:

Review any words missed. Send words to review home for additional study. Praise all efforts.

Week 8

Lessons 36-40 - Assess Student's Knowledge

Goal: To review words from Lessons 1–35.

Review Rule:

Review the rules for the first seven weeks.

What Do You Remember?

Give the students the What do you remember? page for Lessons 1-35. Tell them that this page will be used to see what they remember about the words they have studied so far this year. Select an additional four to six Working Words from the list of words added each week. Ask them to listen carefully to each word as you say it, repeat it in a sentence, and say it once again. Follow the procedures for this page as described in the *Introduction* at the beginning of this Teacher's Guide.

(NOTE: If you have kept records of words that each child continues to find difficult, you may want to adjust the words in this unit to fit the needs of the individual child. Replace review words already mastered with those still needing work.)

What do you remember? Lessons 1-35   Name: _____

Write the words your teacher reads.

1. middle
2. Monday
3. letter
4. water
5. math
6. winter
7. such
8. Sunday
9. second
10. men
11. pencil
12. pet
13. smile
14. United States
15. true
16. new
17. believe
18. seen
19. seek
20. we
21. someone
22. forgot
23. bedroom
24. friendship
25. by
26. grade
27. praise
28. trust

Horizons Spelling Grade 2   65

Lesson 36 - Introduce Words

Activities:

1. Give the students Lesson 36.

2. **Activity 1:** Review the long vowel sounds. Ask the students to find the words in the review list that have long vowel sounds. As an aid, have the students circle the word on the list. Check.

   Ask the students to write the long vowel words on the lines provided and to circle carefully the long vowel combination in each word.

3. **Activity 2:** Have the students find and write the four compound words in the review list.

4. **Activity 3:** Ask the students to find two review words that name days of the week. Write them on the lines provided. Check for capital letters.

5. **Activity 4:** Ask the students to find and write the word from the review list that tells what grade they are in.

6. **Activity 5:** Select, or have the students select, six of the CHOICE working words to be reviewed in this unit. The words may be chosen for the class, or on an individual basis according to the needs of the student.

   Ask the students to write the working words on the six lines provided. Have the students write three sentences using as many of the words as they can.

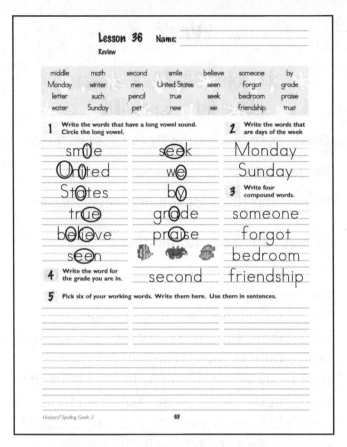

Extended Activities for the Week:

1. Send a list of the week's words home for further study. Emphasize the importance of using spelling words in sentences, in speech, in stories, etc., so that they are given a context and not simply memorized in isolation.

2. Assign reproducible *Week 8 Worksheet* either as homework or as an added classroom activity.

3. Have students review the definitions of the "choice" working words in their notebooks.

4. Review all word family charts.

Lesson 37 - Examine and Explore Words

Activities:

1. Give the students Lesson 37.

2. **Activity 1:** Review short ĕ words. Ask the students to draw a line from the picture to the short ĕ word what matches it.

3. **Activity 2:** Review syllables. Ask the students to find all the two-syllable words (13 in all). Write the two-syllable review words on the lines provided.

4. **Activity 3:** Each sentence in this activity has one review word misspelled. Ask the students to find the word, circle it, and then write the correct spelling on the lines provided below the sentences.

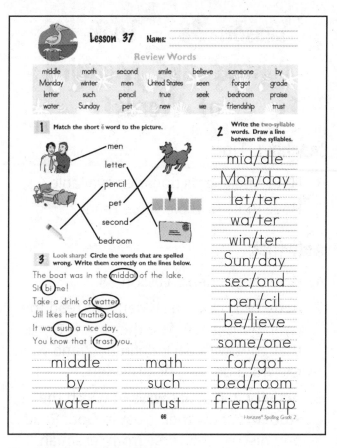

Extended Activities:

1. Check for any difficulties with syllables, and provide additional practice.

2. Check for difficulties with the misspelled words and provide additional help.

Lesson 38 - Look at Context and Meaning of Words

Teaching Tips:

1. Have Spelling dictionaries available.
2. Have Bible or Bible verse ready.

Activities:

1. Give the students Lesson 38.
2. **Activity 1:** Ask the students to read the definitions given, find the review word that goes with each definition, and write the word on the line provided.
3. **Activity 2:** Discuss ways in which the students show their trust in God. Read and discuss the verse from Jeremiah. Ask the students to write the verse and share it with a friend.

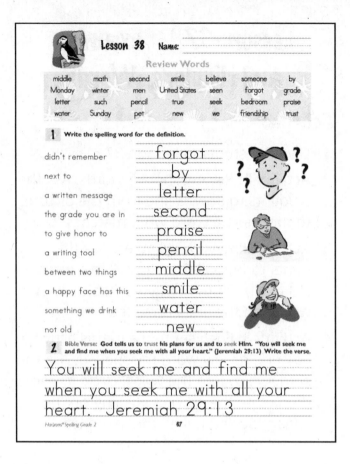

Lesson 39 - Apply Understanding of Words in Writing

Teaching Tip:

Have Spelling dictionaries available.

Activities:

1. Give the students Lesson 39.

2. **Writing Activity:** Begin this page by standing in front of the students with a frown on your face. Note the students' reactions. Switch to a smile and see how they react. Read the directions and discuss them with the students. Share times when students have been affected by a person's smile or frown. Have the students write a story about a smile that helped someone in time of need. Have them draw a picture to go with the story.

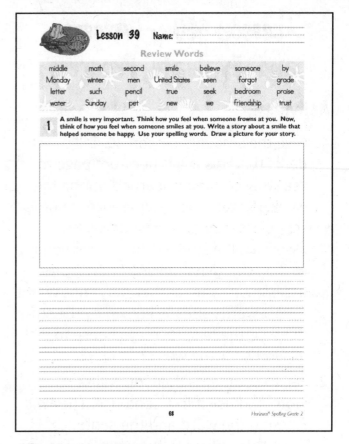

Extended Activity:

Share stories and experiences.

Lesson 40 - Assess and Evaluate Progress

Activities:

1. Give the students Lesson 40. Tell the students that this is a "Check-up" page to see what they have learned during the week. [**Note:** Teachers/parents of home schoolers may decide what will be assessed. If a student does exceptionally well on the "What do you know?" pre-assessment, the teacher may choose not to test words already known by the student. Or the teacher may choose to test all words for the week.]

2. Tell the students that you will say a word and use it in a sentence. They will listen to the word and the sentence. Then they will write the word on the line next to the numbers. All working words are included in this review.

3. Say the word. Repeat it in the context of a sentence. Repeat the word.

4. The students write the word dictated.

5. The process is repeated until all words have been tested.

6. The teacher may correct in class by writing the words on the board and having the students compare or "self-correct" their work. Or the teacher may correct each student's work individually.

7. The teacher then writes any corrections for words misspelled in the space provided.

8. The students study the misspelled words, then practice them on the second side of the Lesson page.

9. Space is provided for retesting, for testing additional sight or "working words" added for the week, and for additional practice.

Check-up Time! Lesson 40 Name: _____

Write the words your teacher reads.

1. _____ 18. _____
2. _____ 19. _____
3. _____ 20. _____
4. _____ 21. _____
5. _____ 22. _____
6. _____ 23. _____
7. _____ 24. _____
8. _____ 25. _____
9. _____ 26. _____
10. _____ 27. _____
11. _____ 28. _____
12. _____
13. _____
14. _____
15. _____
16. _____
17. _____

Horizons® Spelling Grade 2 69

Extended Activity:

Review any words missed. Send words to review home for additional study. Praise all efforts.

Week 9

Lessons 41-45 - Assess Student's Knowledge

Goal: To recognize and spell words with the consonant digraphs **sh**, **ch**, **wh**, **th**.

Review Rules:

A consonant digraph is two or more consonants that stay together to make their special sound. Examples: **shoe**, **show**, **shirt**; **the**, **that**, **three**.

The consonant digraph **ch** makes the sound as in the beginning of **chair**. Examples: **chair**, **choose**, **kitchen**, **watch**, **stitch**.

The **ch** can also make the **k** sound. Example: **chorus**.

In consonant digraph **wh**, the **wh** makes the **w** sound. Examples: **what**, **when**.

What Do You Know?

Give the students the What do you know? page for Lessons 41-45. Tell them that this page will be used to see what they already know about the words for the week. Ask them to listen carefully to each word as you say it, repeat it in a sentence, and say it once again. Follow the procedures for this page as described in the *Introduction* at the beginning of this Teacher's Guide.

Show the children how to write their working words in the appropriate section at the back of their *Spelling Dictionary*.

What do you know?	Lessons 41-45	Name:
Words for the Week	**Corrections**	**Practice**

1. shine
2. wish
3. shout
4. think
5. thimble
6. both
7. why
8. whisper
9. whose
10. while
11. chick
12. chill
13. chime
14. each
15. rich
16. November
17. eighth

Horizons Spelling Grade 2   71

Week 9: Consonant Digraphs

A consonant digraph is two or more consonants that stay together to make their special sound.

Examples: shoe, three, chair, watch, when

Horizons® Spelling Grade 2   163

Lesson 41 - Introduce Words

Activities:

1. Give the students Lesson 41.

2. Write the consonant digraphs **sh**, **th**, **wh**, and **ch** on the board. Have the students dictate words for each digraph. Write them. Encourage words which have the digraphs at both the beginning and the end of the words.

3. **Activity 1:** Have the students look at their spelling words for the week. Ask them to find the words with the consonant digraphs and write them in the appropriate column.

4. **Activity 2:** Write the working words chosen for the week on the board. Ask the students to write all five of their working words for the week on the lines provided.

5. **Activity 3:** Students will write their working words in their Spelling dictionaries in the back section. Words are to be written under the correct letter of the alphabet.

Extended Activities for the Week:

1. Send a list of the week's words home for further study. Emphasize the importance of using spelling words in sentences, in speech, in stories, etc., so that they are given a context and not simply memorized in isolation.

2. Assign reproducible *Week 9 Worksheet* either as homework or as an added classroom activity.

3. Have students write the definitions of the "choice" working words in their notebooks.

4. Have the students begin the writing of sentences for each spelling word in their notebooks.

5. Bring out or begin word family charts for each of the consonant digraphs: **sh**, **ch**, **wh**, and **th**. Charts should include words which have the digraphs at the beginning, middle, or end.

Lesson 42 - Examine and Explore Words

Teaching Tips:

1. Have Spelling dictionaries available.
2. Have word cards for the week available for the ABC order activity.

Activities:

1. Give the students Lesson 42.
2. **Activity 1:** Use one of the CHOICE working words in a sentence.
3. **Activity 2:** Review ABC order. In this activity, some words require looking to the fourth letter to determine the order. Do this activity together as a class. Put the four words in the group on the board. Have the students arrange them in the correct order, then copy them onto the lines provided. Have them draw a line under the letter that helped them find the correct order (second, third, fourth). Check to see that all have the correct order.
4. Using the *Spelling Dictionary*, Have the students look up the words **thimble** and **chime** in their dictionaries. Ask them to read the definition and the model sentence for each. Then have the students write an original sentence for each word on the lines provided.

Extended Activities:

1. Have sets of word cards for the students to practice the ABC order activity. Give additional practice as needed.
2. Have the students continue the writing of sentences for each spelling word in their notebooks.

Lesson 43 - Look at Context and Meaning of Words

Teaching Tips:

1. Have Spelling dictionaries available.
2. Have Bible ready for story.

Activities:

1. Give the students Lesson 43.

2. **Activity 1:** Ask the students to read each sentence aloud trying each of the word choices given. Circle the spelling word that completes the sentence correctly and write the spelling word on the line provided.

3. **Activity 2:** Read the Bible story to the students and discuss it. Talk about how silently God can speak to them in their hearts. Have the students draw a picture for the story and write a sentence using the spelling word.

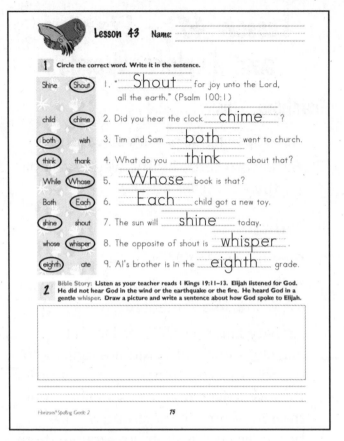

Extended Activities:

1. Expand Bible activity. Connect with Matthew 6:6ff. Spend a little quiet time, just listening and talking quietly to God.

2. Have the students continue the writing of sentences for each spelling word in their notebooks.

Lesson 44 - Apply Understanding of Words in Writing

Teaching Tips:

1. Have Spelling dictionaries available.
2. Have some pictures of occasions for shouting/whispering available.

Activities:

1. Give the students Lesson 44.
2. **Writing Activity:** This activity gives the students the opportunity to write two short stories. Talk about times when people shout and times when people need to whisper. Have the students write their own time to shout and time to whisper in the spaces provided. Have them draw a picture to go with each.

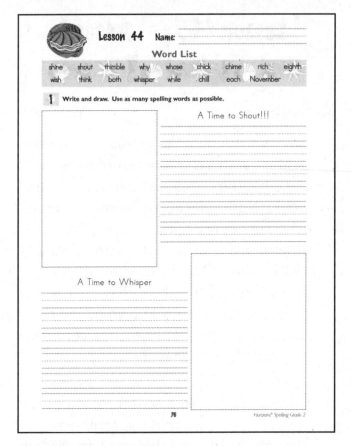

Extended Activities:

1. Share stories and experiences with the class.
2. Have the students complete the writing of sentences for each spelling word in their notebooks.

Lesson 45 - Assess and Evaluate Progress

Activities:

1. Give the students Lesson 45. Tell the students that this is a "Check-up" page to see what they have learned during the week. [**Note:** Teachers/parents of home schoolers may decide what will be assessed. If a student does exceptionally well on the "What do you know?" pre-assessment, the teacher may choose not to test words already known by the student. Or the teacher may choose to test all words for the week.]

2. Tell the students that you will say a word and use it in a sentence. They will listen to the word and the sentence. Then they will write the word on the line next to the numbers. All working words are included in this review.

3. Say the word. Repeat it in the context of a sentence. Repeat the word.

4. The students write the word dictated.

5. The process is repeated until all words have been tested.

6. The teacher may correct in class by writing the words on the board and having the students compare or "self-correct" their work. Or the teacher may correct each student's work individually.

7. The teacher then writes any corrections for words misspelled in the space provided.

8. The students study the misspelled words, then practice them on the second side of the Lesson page.

9. Space is provided for retesting, for testing additional sight or "working words" added for the week, and for additional practice.

Check-up Time! | Lesson 45   Name: _____

Spelling Test

1. _____   11. _____
2. _____   12. _____
3. _____   13. _____
4. _____   14. _____
5. _____   15. _____
6. _____   16. _____
7. _____   17. _____
8. _____   18. _____
9. _____   19. _____
10. _____   20. _____

Corrections

Horizons Spelling Grade 2   77

Extended Activity:

Review any words missed. Send words to review home for additional study. Praise all efforts.

Week 10

Lessons 46-50 - Assess Student's Knowledge

Goal: To recognize contractions and the words they represent.

Review Rules:

Contraction: a short way to write two words as one.

When the two words are put together, one or more letters are left out.

A sign called an apostrophe (') is used to show where the letters were left out.

What Do You Know?

Give the students the What do you know? page for Lessons 46-50. Tell them that this page will be used to see what they already know about the words for the week. Ask them to listen carefully to each word as you say it, repeat it in a sentence, and say it once again. Follow the procedures for this page as described in the *Introduction* at the beginning of this Teacher's Guide.

Show the children how to write their working words in the appropriate section at the back of their *Spelling Dictionary*.

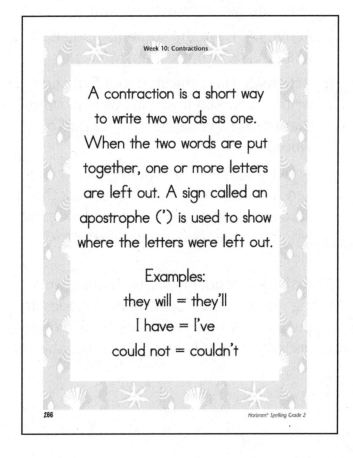

Words for the Week	Corrections	Practice
1. didn't	1.	1.
2. I'd	2.	2.
3. we've	3.	3.
4. weren't	4.	4.
5. you've	5.	5.
6. it's	6.	6.
7. he'll	7.	7.
8. they'll	8.	8.
9. couldn't	9.	9.
10. shouldn't	10.	10.
11. wouldn't	11.	11.
12. won't	12.	12.
13. they've	13.	13.
14. she's	14.	14.
15. he'd	15.	15.
16. Thursday	16.	16.
17. ninth	17.	17.

Horizons Spelling Grade 2   79

Week 10: Contractions

A contraction is a short way to write two words as one. When the two words are put together, one or more letters are left out. A sign called an apostrophe (') is used to show where the letters were left out.

Examples:
they will = they'll
I have = I've
could not = couldn't

166   *Horizons® Spelling Grade 2*

Lesson 46 - Introduce Words

Activities:

1. Give the students Lesson 46.

2. Review the rules for contractions. Write the word "contractions" on the board. Ask the students to give you as many contractions as they can. Write them in groups: **-n't, -'s, -'ll, -'d, -'ve**, etc.

3. Review the list of contractions for the spelling words. How many did the students identify on the board?

4. **Activity 1:** Have the students find the six contractions with **n't** and write them on the lines provided.

5. **Activity 2:** Have the students find and write the three contractions with **'ve**.

6. **Activity 3:** Have the students find and write the two contractions with **'ll**.

7. **Activity 4:** Have the students find and write the two contractions with **'s**.

8. **Activity 5:** Have the students find and write the two contractions with **'d**. Note that the **'d** can stand either for **had** or **would**.

9. **Activity 6:** Write the working words chosen for the week on the board. Ask the students to write all five of their working words for the week on the lines provided.

10. **Activity 7:** Students will write their working words in their Spelling dictionaries in the back section. Words are to be written under the correct letter of the alphabet.

Extended Activities for the Week:

1. Send a list of the week's words home for further study. Emphasize the importance of using spelling words in sentences, in speech, in stories, etc., so that they are given a context and not simply memorized in isolation.

2. Assign reproducible *Week 10 Worksheet* either as homework or as an added classroom activity.

3. Have students write the definitions of the "choice" working words in their notebooks.

4. Have the students begin the writing of sentences for each spelling word in their notebooks.

5. Bring out or begin word family charts for contractions.

Lesson 47 - Examine and Explore Words

Activities:

1. Give the students Lesson 47.

2. **Activity 1:** Ask the students to find and write the spelling word that is the name of a day of the week.

3. **Activity 2:** Ask the students to read each sentence. Have them convert the words underlined to contractions. Write the contractions on the line below the underlined words.

Extended Activities:

1. Make a set of cards with all the contractions the students have learned (Spelling 1 and 2). Make a second set of cards which have the two words spelled out for each contraction. The students can use these as a game (like Concentration), as a matching game, as a drill, and so on.

2. Have the students continue the writing of sentences for each spelling word in their notebooks.

Lesson 48 - Apply Understanding of Words in Writing

Teaching Tips:

1. Have Bible ready for verses.
2. Have word chart of ordinal numbers available.

Activities:

1. Give the students Lesson 48.

2. **Activity 1:** This activity not only works with contractions, but with answering questions using complete sentences. Have the students read the question. Ask them to write a response to the question using one of the contractions from their spelling list. **Examples:** We've time to go to the park. She's taller than I am. They'll come with us. It's cold outside.

3. **Activity 2:** This activity reviews the ordinals that the students have learned to spell this year. Ask them to fill in the missing words: **second, fourth, eighth, ninth.** Have them use their dictionaries if needed.

4. **Activity 3:** Read the Bible verse and discuss it. Ask the students to answer the question in a complete sentence. **Example:** Jesus died at the ninth hour.

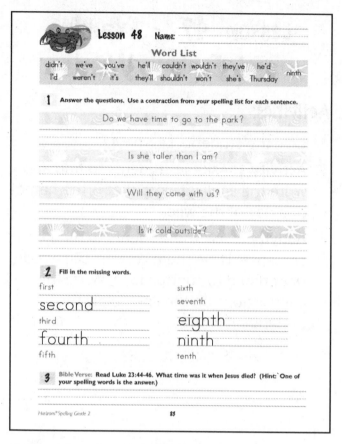

Extended Activities:

1. Give additional practice as needed on contractions.

2. Have the students continue the writing of sentences for each spelling word in their notebooks.

Lesson 49 - Apply Understanding of Words in Writing

Teaching Tip:

Have Spelling dictionaries available.

Activities:

1. Give the students Lesson 49.

2. **Writing Activity:** Discuss various learning situations: a baby learning to walk, learning to read, learning to cook, learning to swim or play ball, etc. Ask the students about situations where they thought they would never be able to learn how to do something. What happened when they tried to learn or when they practiced?

3. Read the directions and discuss. Ask the students to write about one of the times when they thought they simply couldn't do something, but later found that with practice, they could do it and now do it very well. Have them illustrate their stories.

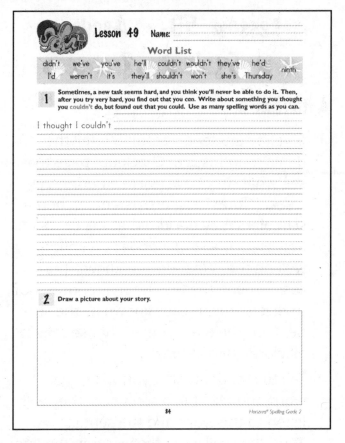

Extended Activities:

1. Share stories and experiences.

2. Have the students complete the writing of sentences for each spelling word in their notebooks.

Lesson 50 - Assess and Evaluate Progress

Activities:

1. Give the students Lesson 50. Tell the students that this is a "Check-up" page to see what they have learned during the week. [**Note:** Teachers/parents of home schoolers may decide what will be assessed. If a student does exceptionally well on the "What do you know?" pre-assessment, the teacher may choose not to test words already known by the student. Or the teacher may choose to test all words for the week.]

2. Tell the students that you will say a word and use it in a sentence. They will listen to the word and the sentence. Then they will write the word on the line next to the numbers. All working words are included in this review.

3. Say the word. Repeat it in the context of a sentence. Repeat the word.

4. The students write the word dictated.

5. The process is repeated until all words have been tested.

6. The teacher may correct in class by writing the words on the board and having the students compare or "self-correct" their work. Or the teacher may correct each student's work individually.

7. The teacher then writes any corrections for words misspelled in the space provided.

8. The students study the misspelled words, then practice them on the second side of the Lesson page.

9. Space is provided for retesting, for testing additional sight or "working words" added for the week, and for additional practice.

Spelling Test

1. _____ 11. _____
2. _____ 12. _____
3. _____ 13. _____
4. _____ 14. _____
5. _____ 15. _____
6. _____ 16. _____
7. _____ 17. _____
8. _____ 18. _____
9. _____ 19. _____
10. _____ 20. _____

Corrections

Horizons® Spelling Grade 2   85

Extended Activity:

Review any words missed. Send words to review home for additional study. Praise all efforts.

Week 11

Lessons 51-55 - Assess Student's Knowledge

Goal: To recognize and spell the plurals of words ending in **-s**, **-es**. To recognize and spell correctly the plural of words ending in **-fe**.

Review Rules:

Plural means "more than one."

Many plurals are formed by adding **-s** to the word. Example: **trucks**, **cars**, **plates**, **things**.

If a word ends in **ss**, **x**, **ch**, or **sh**, add the suffix **-es** to make the word plural.

If a word ends in **f** or **fe**, usually change the **f** or **fe** to **v** before adding the suffix **-es**.

When a word ends in **y** after a consonant, usually change the **y** to an **i** before adding **-es**.

What Do You Know?

Give the students the What do you know? page for Lessons 51-55. Tell them that this page will be used to see what they already know about the words for the week. Ask them to listen carefully to each word as you say it, repeat it in a sentence, and say it once again. Follow the procedures for this page as described in the *Introduction* at the beginning of this Teacher's Guide.

Show the children how to write their working words in the appropriate section at the back of their *Spelling Dictionary*.

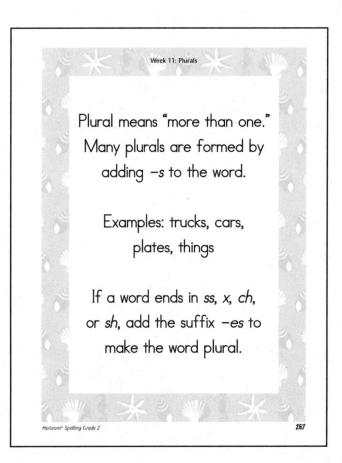

Lesson 51 - Introduce Words

Activities:

1. Give the students Lesson 51.

2. **Activity 1:** Review the rules for forming plurals. Ask the students to follow the directions for each word in this activity and form and write the spelling word for each word puzzle.

3. **Activity 2:** Write the working words chosen for the week on the board. Ask the students to write all five of their working words for the week on the lines provided.

4. **Activity 3:** Students will write their working words in their Spelling dictionaries in the back section. Words are to be written under the correct letter of the alphabet.

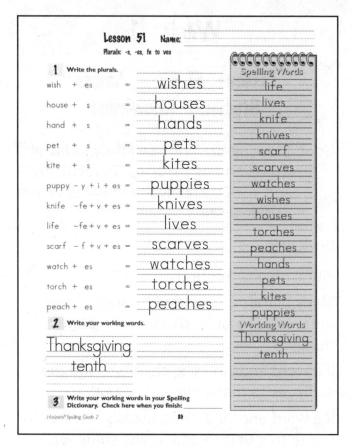

Extended Activities for the Week:

1. Send a list of the week's words home for further study. Emphasize the importance of using spelling words in sentences, in speech, in stories, etc., so that they are given a context and not simply memorized in isolation.

2. Assign reproducible *Week 11 Worksheet* either as homework or as an added classroom activity.

3. Have students write the definitions of the "choice" working words in their notebooks.

4. Have the students begin the writing of sentences for each spelling word in their notebooks.

5. Bring out or begin individual word family charts for regular plurals (adding **s**); plurals of words ending in **ss, x, ch, sh** (adding **es**); plurals ending in **f, fe** (change to **v + es**); plurals ending in **y** (change **y** to **i** and add **es**).

Lesson 52 - Examine and Explore Words

Teaching Tip:

Have 3" x 5" note cards or pieces of paper to aid students with visual discrimination problems with the puzzle.

Activities:

1. Give the students Lesson 52.

2. **Puzzle Activity:** (Provide cards or paper for students who may have visual discrimination problems.) Tell the students that ALL of their spelling words are hidden in this word search puzzle. Some words will go across the lines, and some will go from the top to the bottom of the puzzle. Help as needed.

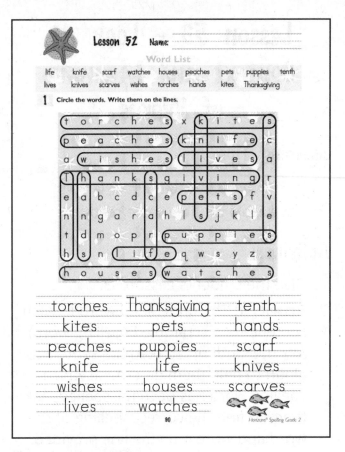

Extended Activities:

1. Provide additional word search practice for students needing further practice.

2. Have the students continue the writing of sentences for each spelling word in their notebooks.

Lesson 53 - Look at Context and Meaning of Words

Teaching Tips:

1. Have Spelling dictionaries available.
2. Have Bible or Bible verse ready.

Activities:

1. Give the students Lesson 53.
2. **Activity 1:** The underlined word in each sentence is a scrambled spelling word. Ask the students to read the sentences aloud to help them determine which spelling word has been misspelled. Ask them to find the correct spelling of the word and write it on the line provided.
3. **Activity 2:** Read Psalms 100:4-5 with the students. Ask the students to write one or two sentences about things they thank God for.

Extended Activities:

1. For students with difficulties, have individual letter cards or tiles at hand so that they can manually rearrange the letters until they find the scrambled words.
2. Have the students continue the writing of sentences for each spelling word in their notebooks.

Lesson 54 - Apply Understanding of Words in Writing

Teaching Tip:

Have Spelling dictionaries available.

Activities:

1. Give the students Lesson 54.

2. **Writing Activity:** Ask the students what they would wish for if they were each given three wishes. Discuss. Have the students decide on three things they would wish for and write about each. Ask them to draw a picture for each wish.

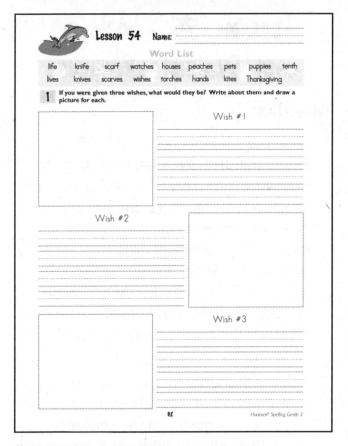

Extended Activities:

1. Share stories and pictures.

2. Have the students complete the writing of sentences for each spelling word in their notebooks.

Lesson 55 - Assess and Evaluate Progress

Activities:

1. Give the students Lesson 55. Tell the students that this is a "Check-up" page to see what they have learned during the week. [**Note:** Teachers/parents of home schoolers may decide what will be assessed. If a student does exceptionally well on the "What do you know?" pre-assessment, the teacher may choose not to test words already known by the student. Or the teacher may choose to test all words for the week.]

2. Tell the students that you will say a word and use it in a sentence. They will listen to the word and the sentence. Then they will write the word on the line next to the numbers. All working words are included in this review.

3. Say the word. Repeat it in the context of a sentence. Repeat the word.

4. The students write the word dictated.

5. The process is repeated until all words have been tested.

6. The teacher may correct in class by writing the words on the board and having the students compare or "self-correct" their work. Or the teacher may correct each student's work individually.

7. The teacher then writes any corrections for words misspelled in the space provided.

8. The students study the misspelled words, then practice them on the second side of the Lesson page.

9. Space is provided for retesting, for testing additional sight or "working words" added for the week, and for additional practice.

Extended Activity:

Review any words missed. Send words to review home for additional study. Praise all efforts.

Week 12

Lessons 56-60 - Assess Student's Knowledge

Goal: To recognize and spell correctly words ending with the suffixes -**ful**, -**less** and -**ment**.

What Do You Know?

Give the students the What do you know? page for Lessons 56-60. Tell them that this page will be used to see what they already know about the words for the week. Ask them to listen carefully to each word as you say it, repeat it in a sentence, and say it once again. Follow the procedures for this page as described in the *Introduction* at the beginning of this Teacher's Guide.

Show the children how to write their working words in the appropriate section at the back of their *Spelling Dictionary*.

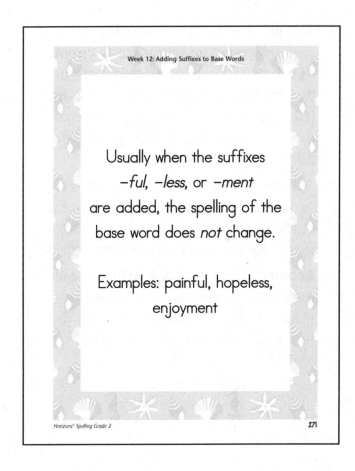

What do you know? Lessons 56-60	Name:	
Words for the Week	**Corrections**	**Practice**
1. thankful		1.
2. helpful		2.
3. handful		3.
4. grateful		4.
5. tearful		5.
6. truthful		6.
7. hopeless		7.
8. helpless		8.
9. fearless		9.
10. shoeless		10.
11. enjoyment		11.
12. judgment		12.
13. forgetful		13.
14. useful		14.
15. wonderful		15.
16. December		16.
17. Friday		17.

Horizons Spelling Grade 2 95

Week 12: Adding Suffixes to Base Words

Usually when the suffixes
–ful, –less, or *–ment*
are added, the spelling of the
base word does *not* change.

Examples: painful, hopeless,
enjoyment

Horizons® Spelling Grade 2 271

Lesson 56 – Introduce Words

Activities:

1. Give the students Lesson 56.

2. Review the rules for suffixes.

3. **Activity 1:** Read the directions with the students. Discuss the two meanings of the suffix **-ful** with the students using the spelling words as an example. You may want to write two columns on the board, the first labeled "full of" and the second for "able to." Take each of the words and discuss its meaning, then write it under the correct column. Example: **wonderful** = full of wonder; **useful** = able to be used. When you have completed this preparation, have the students write the complete words in this activity.

4. **Activity 2:** Read the directions and discuss the meaning of the suffix **-ment**. Ask the students to find and write the two spelling words with the suffix **-ment**. [**Note:** The spelling of **judgment** changes the base word: the **e** is dropped before adding the suffix **-ment**.]

5. **Activity 3:** Write the working words chosen for the week on the board. Ask the students to write all five of their working words for the week on the lines provided.

6. **Activity 4:** Students will write their working words in their Spelling dictionaries in the back section. Words are to be written under the correct letter of the alphabet.

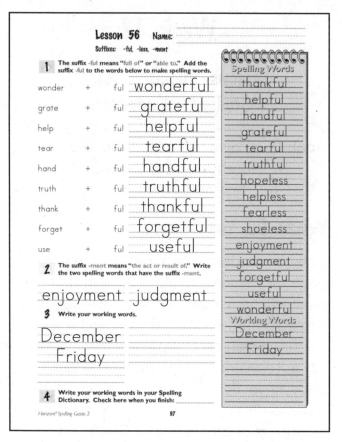

Extended Activities for the Week:

1. Send a list of the week's words home for further study. Emphasize the importance of using spelling words in sentences, in speech, in stories, etc., so that they are given a context and not simply memorized in isolation.

2. Assign reproducible *Week 12 Worksheet* either as homework or as an added classroom activity.

3. Have students write the definitions of the "choice" working words in their notebooks.

4. Have the students begin the writing of sentences for each spelling word in their notebooks.

5. Bring out or begin individual word family charts for words adding the suffix **-ful, -less, -ment**.

Lesson 57 - Examine and Explore Words

Teaching Tips:

1. Have Spelling dictionaries available.
2. Have calendar or chart with names of the days of the week.

Activities:

1. Give the students Lesson 57.

2. **Activity 1:** Read and discuss the directions with the students. Talk about the two meanings of the suffix **-less**. Have the students decide which meaning fits each of the four spelling words in this lesson. Example: **shoeless** = without shoes, **helpless** = unable to do something [could also mean "without help"].

3. **Activity 2:** Review word syllables. Have the students clap the syllables for each word in the lesson. Then ask them to find and write the four three-syllable words on the lines provided.

4. **Activity 3:** The students have now learned to spell the names of all the days of the week. This activity reviews those spellings. Have the students use their Spelling dictionaries if they need help. The first letter(s) of each word are given.

5. **Activity 4:** Review sorting of words in ABC order. Remind the students that sometimes they need to go to the second, third, fourth, or even fifth letter to find the order: **helpful**, **helpless**.

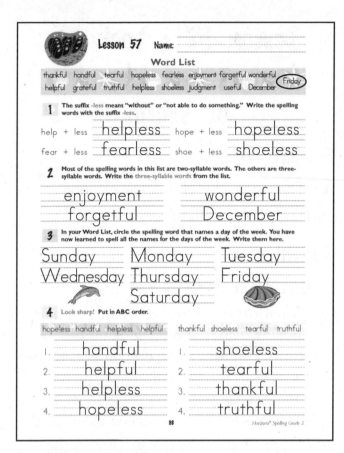

Extended Activities:

1. Provide additional practice for those who need it with writing the days of the week and with sorting in ABC order.

2. Have the students continue the writing of sentences for each spelling word in their notebooks.

Lesson 58 - Look at Context and Meaning of Words

Teaching Tips:

1. Have Spelling dictionaries available.
2. Have Bible or Bible verse ready.

Activities:

1. Give the students Lesson 58.

2. **Activity 1:** Have the students use their Spelling dictionaries to look up the words **judgment** and **enjoyment**. Have them read the definition and the model sentence for each. Ask them to write a sentence of their own using each word.

3. **Activity 2:** Read John 5:30. Discuss the fact that only Jesus knows hearts and can judge them—we cannot! Read the directions and ask the students to write ways they can be pleasing to God. Use as many of the words in the box as possible.

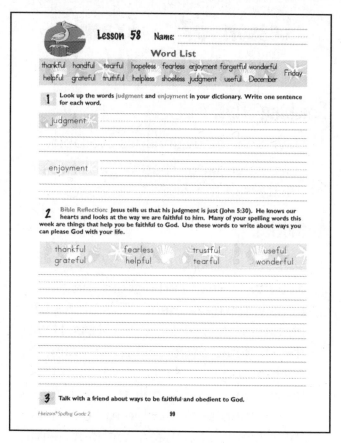

Extended Activities:

1. Share the Bible reflections. Perhaps the students can expand on them and make a bulletin board of their ideas.

2. Have the students continue the writing of sentences for each spelling word in their notebooks.

Lesson 59 - Apply Understanding of Words in Writing

Teaching Tips:

1. Have Spelling dictionaries available.
2. Have Christmas pictures or other December pictures available.

Activities:

1. Give the students Lesson 59.
2. **Writing Activity:** Since this lesson will most likely come in December, ask the students to write about the special birthday Christians celebrate in December. Use as many spelling words as possible.

Extended Activities:

1. Share stories. Have students expand and illustrate them.
2. Have the students complete the writing of sentences for each spelling word in their notebooks.

Lesson 60 - Assess and Evaluate Progress

Activities:

1. Give the students Lesson 60. Tell the students that this is a "Check-up" page to see what they have learned during the week. [**Note:** Teachers/parents of home schoolers may decide what will be assessed. If a student does exceptionally well on the "What do you know?" pre-assessment, the teacher may choose not to test words already known by the student. Or the teacher may choose to test all words for the week.]

2. Tell the students that you will say a word and use it in a sentence. They will listen to the word and the sentence. Then they will write the word on the line next to the numbers. All working words are included in this review.

3. Say the word. Repeat it in the context of a sentence. Repeat the word.

4. The students write the word dictated.

5. The process is repeated until all words have been tested.

6. The teacher may correct in class by writing the words on the board and having the students compare or "self-correct" their work. Or the teacher may correct each student's work individually.

7. The teacher then writes any corrections for words misspelled in the space provided.

8. The students study the misspelled words, then practice them on the second side of the Lesson page.

9. Space is provided for retesting, for testing additional sight or "working words" added for the week, and for additional practice.

What do you know? Lesson 60 Name: _____

Spelling Test

1. _____	11. _____
2. _____	12. _____
3. _____	13. _____
4. _____	14. _____
5. _____	15. _____
6. _____	16. _____
7. _____	17. _____
8. _____	18. _____
9. _____	19. _____
10. _____	20. _____

Corrections

Horizons® Spelling Grade 2   101

Extended Activity:

Review any words missed. Send words to review home for additional study. Praise all efforts.

Week 13

Lessons 61-65 - Assess Student's Knowledge

Goal: To recognize and spell words ending in **-ing**, **-ong**, **-ung**, **-ang**.

What Do You Know?

Give the students the What do you know? page for Lessons 61-65. Tell them that this page will be used to see what they already know about the words for the week. Ask them to listen carefully to each word as you say it, repeat it in a sentence, and say it once again. Follow the procedures for this page as described in the *Introduction* at the beginning of this Teacher's Guide.

Show the children how to write their working words in the appropriate section at the back of their *Spelling Dictionary*.

What do you know? Lessons 61-65	Name:	
Words for the Week	**Corrections**	**Practice**
1. rang		1.
2. sang		2.
3. hang		3.
4. clang		4.
5. thing		5.
6. ring		6.
7. sing		7.
8. wing		8.
9. song		9.
10. strong		10.
11. swing		11.
12. string		12.
13. rung		13.
14. sung		14.
15. lung		15.
16. sixth		16.
17. seventh		17.

Horizons Spelling Grade 2   105

Lesson 61 - Introduce Words

Activities:

1. Give the students Lesson 61.

2. **Activity 1:** Review rhymes with the students. Have them find and write the spelling words for each group given.

3. **Activity 2:** Write the working words chosen for the week on the board. Ask the students to write all five of their working words for the week on the lines provided.

4. **Activity 3:** Students will write their working words in their Spelling dictionaries in the back section. Words are to be written under the correct letter of the alphabet.

Extended Activities:

1. Send a list of the week's words home for further study. Emphasize the importance of using spelling words in sentences, in speech, in stories, etc., so that they are given a context and not simply memorized in isolation.

2. Assign reproducible *Week 13 Worksheet* either as homework or as an added classroom activity.

3. Have students write the definitions of the "choice" working words in their notebooks.

4. Have the students begin the writing of sentences for each spelling word in their notebooks.

5. Bring out or begin individual word family charts for each grouping: **-ing**, **-ong**, **-ang**, **-ung**.

Lesson 62 - Examine and Explore Words

Teaching Tip:

Have list or chart of ordinal numbers available.

Activities:

1. Give the students Lesson 62.

2. **Activity 1:** Review ordinal numbers. The students have now learned to spell these numbers from "first" to "tenth." Ask them to write the word for each number given. Circle the ones that are spelling words: **sixth** and **seventh**. Have the students use their Spelling dictionaries as needed.

3. **Activity 2:** Have the students read the definitions given, find the spelling word in the box for each definition, and write the word on the line provided.

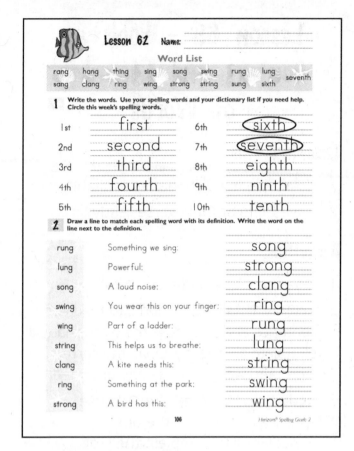

Extended Activities:

1. Give additional practice with ordinal number words as needed.

2. Have the students continue the writing of sentences for each spelling word in their notebooks.

Lesson 63 - Look at Context and Meaning of Words

Teaching Tips:

1. Have Spelling dictionaries available.
2. Have Bible or Bible verse ready.

Activities:

1. Give the students Lesson 63.
2. **Activity 1:** Ask the students to read each sentence and to choose the word that will complete it correctly. Circle the correct word and write it on the line provided.
3. **Activity 2:** Have the students use spelling words from the box in Activity 1 to complete the story.

Extended Activity:

Have the students continue the writing of sentences for each spelling word in their notebooks.

Lesson 64 - Apply Understanding of Words in Writing

Teaching Tips:

1. Have Spelling dictionaries available.
2. Have Bible ready for Psalm 33:1-5. Mark additional Psalms of praise.

Activities:

1. Give the students Lesson 64.
2. **Writing Activity:** Read Psalm 33:1-5 with the students. Read other psalms of praise if time allows. Ask the students to write their own psalms, songs of praise, in the space provided. Use spelling words if possible. Decorate the page around the song of praise.

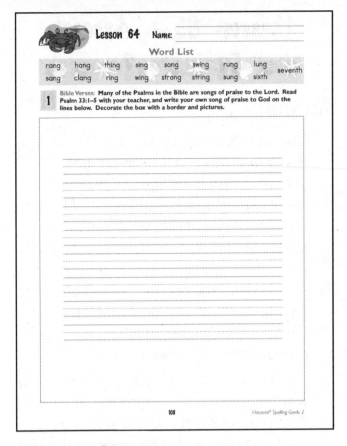

Extended Activities:

1. Share songs of praise with the class.
2. Have the students complete the writing of sentences for each spelling word in their notebooks.

Lesson 65 - Assess and Evaluate Progress

Activities:

1. Give the students Lesson 65. Tell the students that this is a "Check-up" page to see what they have learned during the week. [**Note:** Teachers/parents of home schoolers may decide what will be assessed. If a student does exceptionally well on the "What do you know?" pre-assessment, the teacher may choose not to test words already known by the student. Or the teacher may choose to test all words for the week.]

2. Tell the students that you will say a word and use it in a sentence. They will listen to the word and the sentence. Then they will write the word on the line next to the numbers. All working words are included in this review.

3. Say the word. Repeat it in the context of a sentence. Repeat the word.

4. The students write the word dictated.

5. The process is repeated until all words have been tested.

6. The teacher may correct in class by writing the words on the board and having the students compare or "self-correct" their work. Or the teacher may correct each student's work individually.

7. The teacher then writes any corrections for words misspelled in the space provided.

8. The students study the misspelled words, then practice them on the second side of the Lesson page.

9. Space is provided for retesting, for testing additional sight or "working words" added for the week, and for additional practice.

Check-up Time! Lesson 65 Name: _____

Spelling Test

1.	11.
2.	12.
3.	13.
4.	14.
5.	15.
6.	16.
7.	17.
8.	18.
9.	19.
10.	20.

Corrections

Horizons® Spelling Grade 2   109

Extended Activity:

Review any words missed. Send words to review home for additional study. Praise all efforts.

Week 14

Lessons 66-70 - Assess Student's Knowledge

Goal: To recognize and spell words having the hard and soft **c** sounds. To recognize and spell words having the hard and soft **g** sounds.

Review Rules:

When **c** is followed by **e**, **i**, or **y**, it makes the soft sound, as in the word "**city**." When **c** is followed by **a**, **u**, or **o** or a consonant, it makes the hard sound, as in the word "**cat**."

When **g** is followed by **e**, **i**, or **y**, it makes the soft sound, as in the word "giraffe."

When **g** is followed by **a**, **u**, or **o** or a consonant, it makes the hard sound, as in the word "**gum**."

What Do You Know?

Give the students the What do you know? page for Lessons 66-70. Tell them that this page will be used to see what they already know about the words for the week. Ask them to listen carefully to each word as you say it, repeat it in a sentence, and say it once again. Follow the procedures for this page as described in the *Introduction* at the beginning of this Teacher's Guide.

Show the children how to write their working words in the appropriate section at the back of their *Spelling Dictionary*.

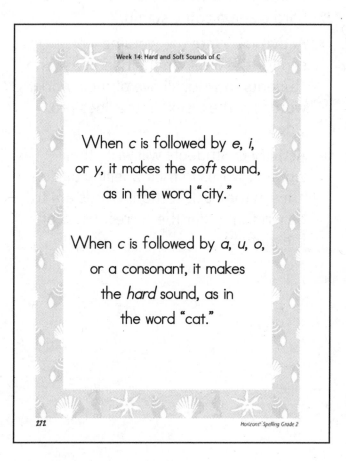

Lesson 66 - Introduce Words

Activities:

1. Give the students Lesson 66.

2. Review hard and soft **c** sounds. Ask the students to give you examples. Write them on the board.

3. **Activity 1:** Ask the students to find and write the five words that begin with hard **c** sound.

4. **Activity 2:** Ask the students to find and write the three words that begin with the soft **c** sound.

5. **Activity 3:** Ask the students to find and write the word that has a soft **c** sound in the middle.

6. **Activity 4:** Ask the students to find and write the two words that have both a hard **c** and a soft **c** sound.

7. **Activity 5:** Write the working words chosen for the week on the board. Ask the students to write all five of their working words for the week on the lines provided.

8. **Activity 6:** Students will write their working words in their Spelling dictionaries in the back section. Words are to be written under the correct letter of the alphabet.

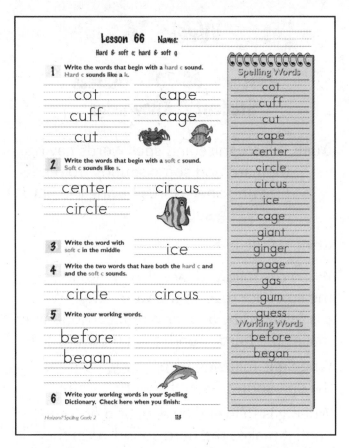

Extended Activities for the Week:

1. Send a list of the week's words home for further study. Emphasize the importance of using spelling words in sentences, in speech, in stories, etc., so that they are given a context and not simply memorized in isolation.

2. Assign reproducible *Week 14 Worksheet* either as homework or as an added classroom activity.

3. Have students write the definitions of the "choice" working words in their notebooks.

4. Have the students begin the writing of sentences for each spelling word in their notebooks.

5. Bring out or begin individual word family charts for hard and soft **c** and **g** sounds.

Lesson 67 - Examine and Explore Words

Activities:

1. Give the students Lesson 67.

2. Review hard and soft **g** sounds. Ask the students for examples. Write them on the board. Refer to the rules for hard and soft **g**.

3. **Activity 1:** Ask the students to find and write the three words that begin with the hard **g** sound.

4. **Activity 2:** Ask the students to find and write the four words that contain the soft **g** sound. [**Note:** Two of the words begin with soft **g** and two do not.] Ask them to circle the one word that has soft **g** used twice.

5. **Activity 3:** Review sorting by ABC order. Remind students that they may have to look as far as the fifth letter to determine the correct order: **circle, circus**.

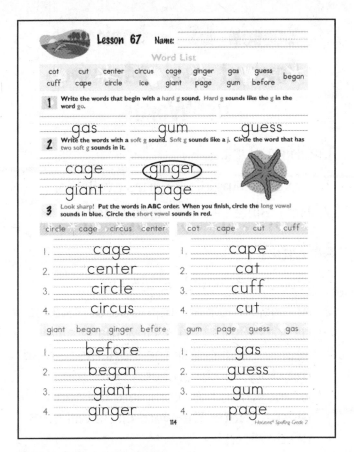

Extended Activities:

1. Provide word cards for this week's spelling words for additional ABC order practice. If students continue to have difficulty, underline the key letter for them as an aid.

2. Have the students continue the writing of sentences for each spelling word in their notebooks.

Horizons Spelling Grade 2

Lesson 68 - Look at Context and Meaning of Words

Teaching Tips:

1. Have Spelling dictionaries available.
2. Have Bible or Bible verse ready.

Activities:

1. Give the students Lesson 68.
2. **Activity 1:** Talk about the students experiences with a circus. How many have seen a circus? Ask the students to read the story and to find and write the words which best complete the sentences. [**Note:** The word **circle** will be used twice.]
3. **Activity 2:** Ask the students to draw a picture of the story.

Extended Activities:

1. Share pictures and circus experiences.
2. Have the students continue the writing of sentences for each spelling word in their notebooks.

Lesson 69 - Apply Understanding of Words in Writing

Teaching Tips:

1. Have Spelling dictionaries available.
2. Have Bible story ready and any pictures of the story you may have.

Activities:

1. Give the students Lesson 69.
2. **Writing Activity:** Read the story of David and Goliath to the students. Ask the students to write about the story in their own words. Have them illustrate the story.

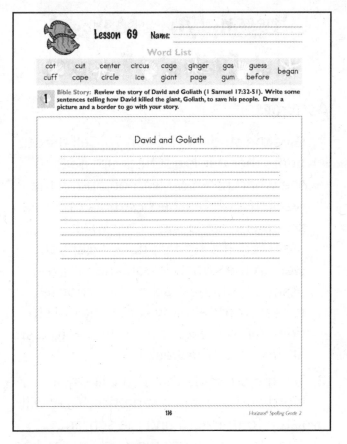

Extended Activities:

1. Share stories and pictures.
2. Act out story if time allows.
3. Have the students complete the writing of sentences for each spelling word in their notebooks.

Lesson 70 - Assess and Evaluate Progress

Activities:

1. Give the students Lesson 70. Tell the students that this is a "Check-up" page to see what they have learned during the week. [**Note:** Teachers/parents of home schoolers may decide what will be assessed. If a student does exceptionally well on the "What do you know?" pre-assessment, the teacher may choose not to test words already known by the student. Or the teacher may choose to test all words for the week.]

2. Tell the students that you will say a word and use it in a sentence. They will listen to the word and the sentence. Then they will write the word on the line next to the numbers. All working words are included in this review.

3. Say the word. Repeat it in the context of a sentence. Repeat the word.

4. The students write the word dictated.

5. The process is repeated until all words have been tested.

6. The teacher may correct in class by writing the words on the board and having the students compare or "self-correct" their work. Or the teacher may correct each student's work individually.

7. The teacher then writes any corrections for words misspelled in the space provided.

8. The students study the misspelled words, then practice them on the second side of the Lesson page.

9. Space is provided for retesting, for testing additional sight or "working words" added for the week, and for additional practice.

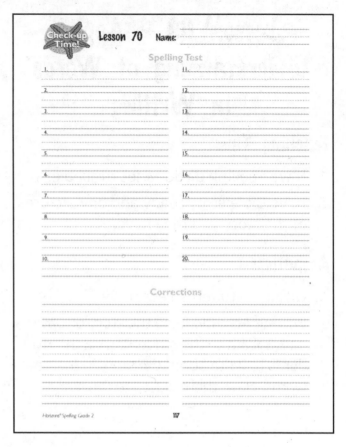

Extended Activity:

Review any words missed. Send words to review home for additional study. Praise all efforts.

Week 15

Lessons 71-75 - Assess Student's Knowledge

Goal: To recognize and spell words having the long and short **oo** sounds.

Review Rules:

Vowel digraphs are two vowels put together in a word that make a long or short sound, or have a special sound all their own.

The vowel digraph **oo** can stand for the vowel sound heard in **book** or in **pool**.

What Do You Know?

Give the students the What do you know? page for Lessons 71-75. Tell them that this page will be used to see what they already know about the words for the week. Ask them to listen carefully to each word as you say it, repeat it in a sentence, and say it once again. Follow the procedures for this page as described in the *Introduction* at the beginning of this Teacher's Guide.

Show the children how to write their working words in the appropriate section at the back of their *Spelling Dictionary*.

What do you know?

Lessons 71-75   Name:

Words for the Week	Corrections	Practice
1. hood		
2. shook		
3. wool		
4. took		
5. stood		
6. cook		
7. wood		
8. boot		
9. spoon		
10. cool		
11. goose		
12. pool		
13. roof		
14. tool		
15. noon		
16. beside		
17. between		

Horizons Spelling Grade 2   118

Week 15: Vowel Digraphs

Vowel digraphs are two vowels put together in a word that make a long or short sound, or have a special sound all their own.

174   *Horizons® Spelling Grade 2*

Lesson 71 - Introduce Words

Activities:

1. Give the students Lesson 71.

2. Make two columns on the board. In the first, review the long sound of **oo** (**moon**, **food**, **zoo**). Have the students give more examples. In the second column, review the short sound of **oo** (**book**, **good**, **foot**). Have the students give more examples.

3. **Activity 1:** Have the students find and write the spelling word for each long **oo** picture.

4. **Activity 2:** Have the students find and write the two spelling words with the long **oo** sound that were not pictured.

5. **Activity 3:** Have the students find and write the spellings words with the short **oo** sound in the correct shapes. Have them circle the **oo**.

6. **Activity 4:** Write the working words chosen for the week on the board. Ask the students to write all five of their working words for the week on the lines provided.

7. **Activity 5:** Students will write their working words in their Spelling dictionaries in the back section. Words are to be written under the correct letter of the alphabet.

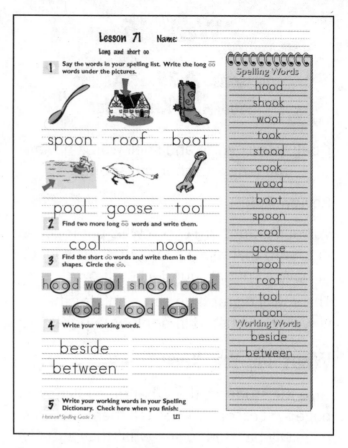

Extended Activities for the Week:

1. Send a list of the week's words home for further study. Emphasize the importance of using spelling words in sentences, in speech, in stories, etc., so that they are given a context and not simply memorized in isolation.

2. Assign reproducible *Week 15 Worksheet* either as homework or as an added classroom activity.

3. Have students write the definitions of the "choice" working words in their notebooks.

4. Have the students begin the writing of sentences for each spelling word in their notebooks.

5. Bring out or begin individual word family charts for the long and short sounds of **oo**.

Lesson 72 - Examine and Explore Words

Activities:

1. Give the students Lesson 72.

2. Review the working of crossword puzzles.

3. **Crossword Activity:** Have the students read the clues for each number. Have them find and write the correct spelling word. Check on students to make sure they are writing the correct word in the correct space.

Extended Activities:

1. Provide additional crossword practice if students are having difficulty.

2. Have the students continue the writing of sentences for each spelling word in their notebooks.

Lesson 73 - Look at Context and Meaning of Words

Teaching Tip:

Have Spelling dictionaries available.

Activities:

1. Give the students Lesson 73.
2. **Activity 1:** Ask the students to read the sentence, choose the word that best completes the sentence, and write the word in the space provided.

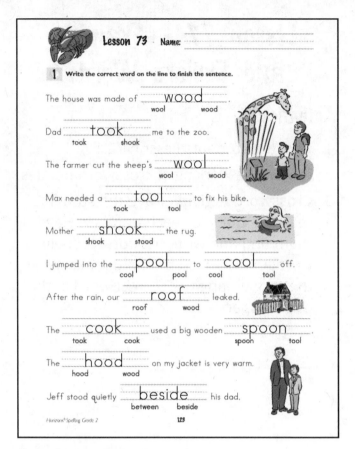

Extended Activity:

Have the students continue the writing of sentences for each spelling word in their notebooks.

Horizons Spelling Grade 2

Lesson 74 - Apply Understanding of Words in Writing

Teaching Tip:

Have Spelling dictionaries available.

Activities:

1. Give the students Lesson 74.

2. **Writing Activity:** Discuss this silly picture with the students. Ask them to write a story about the picture and to color the picture.

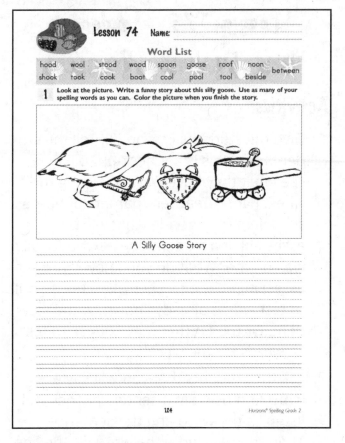

Lesson 74   Name:

Word List

| hood | wool | stood | wood | spoon | goose | roof | noon | between |
| shook | took | cook | boot | cool | pool | tool | beside | |

1 Look at the picture. Write a funny story about this silly goose. Use as many of your spelling words as you can. Color the picture when you finish the story.

A Silly Goose Story

124   Horizons Spelling Grade 2

Extended Activities:

1. Share funny stories.

2. Have the students complete the writing of sentences for each spelling word in their notebooks.

Lesson 75 – Assess and Evaluate Progress

Activities:

1. Give the students Lesson 75. Tell the students that this is a "Check-up" page to see what they have learned during the week. [**Note:** Teachers/parents of home schoolers may decide what will be assessed. If a student does exceptionally well on the "What do you know?" pre-assessment, the teacher may choose not to test words already known by the student. Or the teacher may choose to test all words for the week.]

2. Tell the students that you will say a word and use it in a sentence. They will listen to the word and the sentence. Then they will write the word on the line next to the numbers. All working words are included in this review.

3. Say the word. Repeat it in the context of a sentence. Repeat the word.

4. The students write the word dictated.

5. The process is repeated until all words have been tested.

6. The teacher may correct in class by writing the words on the board and having the students compare or "self-correct" their work. Or the teacher may correct each student's work individually.

7. The teacher then writes any corrections for words misspelled in the space provided.

8. The students study the misspelled words, then practice them on the second side of the Lesson page.

9. Space is provided for retesting, for testing additional sight or "working words" added for the week, and for additional practice.

Check-up Time! Lesson 75 Name: _____

Spelling Test

1.	11.
2.	12.
3.	13.
4.	14.
5.	15.
6.	16.
7.	17.
8.	18.
9.	19.
10.	20.

Corrections

Horizons Spelling Grade 2   115

Extended Activity:

Review any words missed. Send words to review home for additional study. Praise all efforts.

Week 16

Lessons 76-80 - Assess Student's Knowledge

Goal: To review words from Lessons 41-75.

Review Rules:

Review all rules from the last seven weeks.

What Do You Remember?

Give the students the What do you remember? page for Lessons 41-75. Tell them that this page will be used to see what they remember about the words they have studied so far this year. Select an additional four to six Working Words from the list of words added each week. Ask them to listen carefully to each word as you say it, repeat it in a sentence, and say it once again. Follow the procedures for this page as described in the Introduction at the beginning of this Teacher's Guide.

(NOTE: If you have kept records of words that each child continues to find difficult, you may want to adjust the words in this unit to fit the needs of the individual child. Replace review words already mastered with those still needing work.)

Show the children how to write their working words in the appropriate section at the back of their *Spelling Dictionary*.

What do you remember? Lessons 41-75   Name: _____

Write the words your teacher reads.

1. think
2. whose
3. why
4. each
5. we've
6. it's
7. won't
8. didn't
9. life
10. houses
11. puppies
12. lives
13. thankful
14. useful
15. helpless
16. enjoyment
17. sang
18. thing
19. strong
20. rung
21. before
22. began
23. page
24. guess
25. took
26. between
27. beside
28. noon

Horizons Spelling Grade 2   127

Lesson 76 - Introduce Words

Activities:

1. Give the students Lesson 76.

2. **Activity 1:** Have the students find and write the four contractions in the review spelling list.

3. **Activity 2:** Have the students find and write two question words from the list.

4. **Activity 3:** Ask the students to find and write the four words that have suffixes.

5. **Activity 4:** Ask the students to find and write three plural words. Have them tell what is different about the plurals for **puppies** and **life**.

6. **Activity 5:** Ask the students to find and write four words that begin with **be**.

7. **Activity 6:** Select, or have the students select, six of the CHOICE working words to be reviewed in this unit. The words may be chosen for the class or on an individual basis according to the needs of the student. Ask the students to write the working words on the six lines provided.

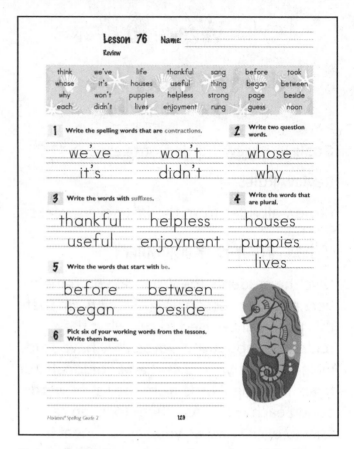

Extended Activities for the Week:

1. Send a list of the week's words home for further study. Emphasize the importance of using spelling words in sentences, in speech, in stories, etc., so that they are given a context and not simply memorized in isolation.

2. Assign reproducible *Week 16 Worksheet* either as homework or as an added classroom activity.

3. Have students review the definitions of the "choice" working words in their notebooks.

4. Bring out word family charts for review.

Lesson 77 - Examine and Explore Words

Activities:

1. Give the students Lesson 77.
2. **Activity 1:** Have the students find and write the spelling word that completes each set of words. Give help as needed. Some associations are more difficult than others.

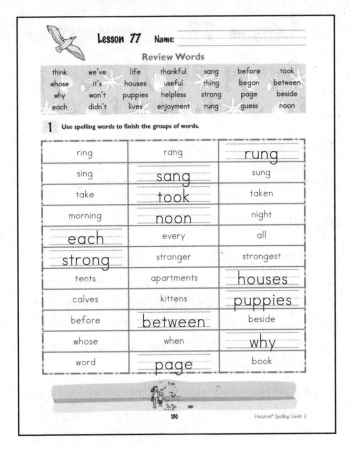

Extended Activity:

Note areas that still need work and give help on an individual basis.

Lesson 78 – Look at Context and Meaning of Words

Teaching Tip:

Have Spelling dictionaries available.

Activities:

1. Give the students Lesson 78.

2. **Activity 1:** Have the students write the words in ABC order. Remind them that they may need to look to the fifth letter in some words to determine the order: **thing**, **think**.

3. **Activity 2:** Ask the students to read each sentence, decide which word or words best complete that sentence, and write the correct word in the space provided.

Lesson 78   Name:

1 Look sharp! **Put in ABC order.**

strong   sang   thing   took   think   thankful

1. sang
2. strong
3. thankful
4. thing
5. think
6. took

2 Write the correct spelling words to complete the sentences.

Before school started, it began to rain.
Beside   Before   between   began

I stood beside my dad.
         beside   between

The new puppies were born yesterday.
        puppies   houses

That cat seems to have nine lives .
                              life   lives

Whose book is that?
Why   Whose

My sister asked me why I was sad.
              why   whose

She didn't want to go with us.
    we've   didn't

I'll meet you at noon for lunch.
              noon   boot

Horizons Spelling Grade 2   191

Lesson 79 - Apply Understanding of Words in Writing

Teaching Tip:

Have Spelling dictionaries available.

Activities:

1. Give the students Lesson 79.

2. **Writing Activity:** Ask the students to use their Spelling dictionaries to look up each word given. Then ask them to write a sentence of their own for each word.

Lesson 79   Name:

1 Use your dictionary. Look up each word. Read the sentence and the definition. Write your own sentence for each word.

guess

useful

strong

each

helpless

beside

enjoyment

between

152   Horizons Spelling Grade 2

Extended Activity:

Share sentences.

Lesson 80 – Assess and Evaluate Progress

Activities:

1. Give the students Lesson 80. Tell the students that this is a "Check-up" page to see what they have learned during the week. [**Note:** Teachers/parents of home schoolers may decide what will be assessed. If a student does exceptionally well on the "What do you know?" pre-assessment, the teacher may choose not to test words already known by the student. Or the teacher may choose to test all words for the week.]

2. Tell the students that you will say a word and use it in a sentence. They will listen to the word and the sentence. Then they will write the word on the line next to the numbers. All working words are included in this review.

3. Say the word. Repeat it in the context of a sentence. Repeat the word.

4. The students write the word dictated.

5. The process is repeated until all words have been tested.

6. The teacher may correct in class by writing the words on the board and having the students compare or "self-correct" their work. Or the teacher may correct each student's work individually.

7. The teacher then writes any corrections for words misspelled in the space provided.

8. The students study the misspelled words, then practice them on the second side of the Lesson page.

9. Space is provided for retesting, for testing additional sight or "working words" added for the week, and for additional practice.

Extended Activity:

Review any words missed. Send words to review home for additional study. Praise all efforts.

Week 17

Lessons 81-85 - Assess Student's Knowledge

Goal: To recognize and spell words with the **ow** (clown), **ow** (low) and **ou** sounds.

Review Rules:

A vowel diphthong is two vowels that blend together to make one sound.

The diphthongs **ow** and **ou** stand for the sounds heard in **out**, and **brown**.

The vowel diphthong **ow** can make two sounds: **ow** as in **cow**, or **ow** as in **snow**.

What Do You Know?

Give the students the What do you know? page for Lessons 81-85. Tell them that this page will be used to see what they already know about the words for the week. Ask them to listen carefully to each word as you say it, repeat it in a sentence, and say it once again. Follow the procedures for this page as described in the *Introduction* at the beginning of this Teacher's Guide.

Show the children how to write their working words in the appropriate section at the back of their *Spelling Dictionary*.

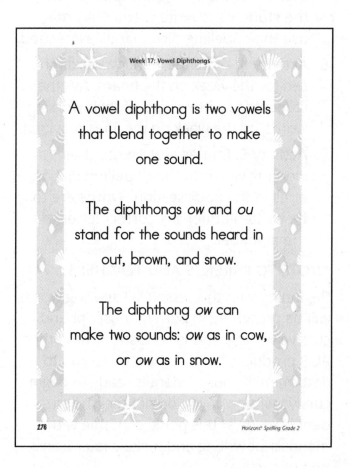

What do you know?	Lessons 81-85	Name:
Words for the Week	**Corrections**	**Practice**

1. cloud
2. count
3. found
4. mouth
5. south
6. clown
7. how
8. town
9. wow
10. plow
11. grow
12. low
13. slow
14. row
15. blow
16. January
17. beyond

Horizons Spelling Grade 2 — 195

Week 17: Vowel Diphthongs

A vowel diphthong is two vowels that blend together to make one sound.

The diphthongs *ow* and *ou* stand for the sounds heard in out, brown, and snow.

The diphthong *ow* can make two sounds: *ow* as in cow, or *ow* as in snow.

276 — *Horizons® Spelling Grade 2*

Lesson 81 - Introduce Words

Activities:

1. Give the students Lesson 81.*

2. Put three columns on the board: **ow** (as in **cow**), **ow** (as in **bowl**), **ou** (as in **out**). Point out that the **ow** in **cow** and the **ou** in **out** have the same sound. Ask the students for additional words for each column.

3. **Activity 1:** Ask the students to find and write the five spelling words that have the **ou** sound.

4. **Activity 2:** Ask the students to find and write the spelling word that names the first month of the year.

5. **Activity 3:** Review all the names of months of the year learned to date. Ask the students to write them. They may use their Spelling dictionaries as needed.

6. **Activity 4:** Write the working words chosen for the week on the board. Ask the students to write all five of their working words for the week on the lines provided.

7. **Activity 5:** Students will write their working words in their Spelling dictionaries in the back section. Words are to be written under the correct letter of the alphabet.

*NOTE TO PARENTS AND TEACHERS:

Beginning with this lesson, all spelling words will be presented in both manuscript and cursive writing. This is consistent with other AOP products; however, it is up to you to determine if your student is ready to begin cursive writing. If you do not feel the student is ready at this point, continue with manuscript writing and make a later transition to cursive.

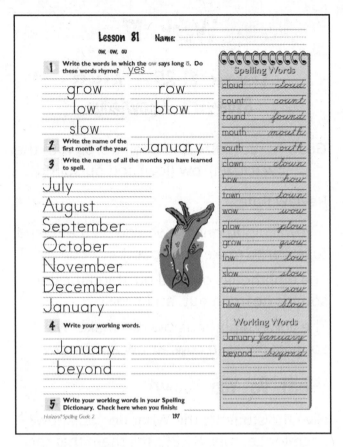

Extended Activities for the Week:

1. Send a list of the week's words home for further study. Emphasize the importance of using spelling words in sentences, in speech, in stories, etc., so that they are given a context and not simply memorized in isolation

2. Assign reproducible *Week 17 Worksheet* either as homework or as an added classroom activity.

3. Have students write the definitions of the "choice" working words in their notebooks.

4. Have the students begin the writing of sentences for each spelling word in their notebooks.

5. Bring out or begin individual word family charts for the **ow, ou** sounds.

Lesson 82 - Examine and Explore Words

Teaching Tip:

Have Spelling dictionaries available.

Activities:

1. Give the students Lesson 82.
2. **Activity 1:** Have the students find and write the **ow** spelling words in the correct box.
3. **Activity 2:** Ask the students to find and write the two **ou** words that rhyme.
4. **Activity 3:** Most of the words in this lesson are one-syllable words. Ask the students to find the two-syllable word (**beyond**) and write it in a sentence. Circle the word.
5. **Activity 4:** Ask the students to select two of their CHOICE working words to use in a sentence.

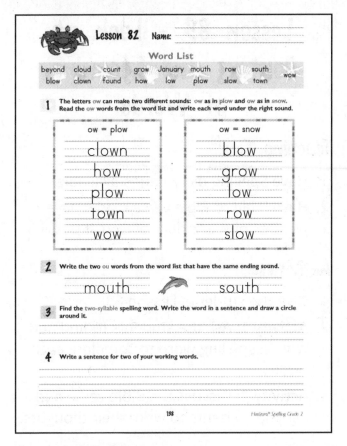

Extended Activities:

1. Provide additional practice with both word and picture cards for sorting out the two sounds of **ow**.
2. Have the students continue the writing of sentences for each spelling word in their notebooks.

Lesson 83 - Look at Context and Meaning of Words

Teaching Tips:

1. Have Spelling dictionaries available.
2. Have Bible or Bible verse ready. Have pictures of the "cloud" of God, if possible.

Activities:

1. Give the students Lesson 83.
2. **Activity 1:** Ask the students to find and write a spelling word to complete each riddle.
3. **Activity 2:** Discuss the Bible verse and ask the students to write their thoughts.

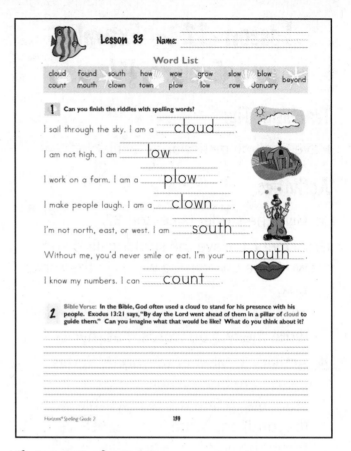

Extended Activities:

1. Share thoughts written by the students.
2. Have the students copy and illustrate the verse.
3. Have the students continue the writing of sentences for each spelling word in their notebooks.

Lesson 84 - Apply Understanding of Words in Writing

Teaching Tips:

1. Have Spelling dictionaries available.
2. Have cloud pictures available.

Activities:

1. Give the students Lesson 84.
2. **Writing Activity:** Do some brainstorming with the students. If the day happens to be one with big, puffy white clouds, let them look out the window or go outside for a few minutes to see what shapes they can find. Ask them to write and illustrate a story about cloud shapes they have seen.

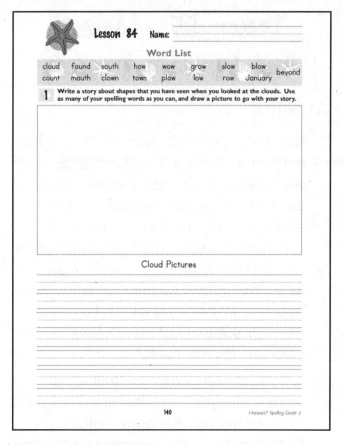

Extended Activities:

1. Share stories and illustrations.
2. Have the students complete the writing of sentences for each spelling word in their notebooks.

Lesson 85 - Assess and Evaluate Progress

Activities:

1. Give the students Lesson 85. Tell the students that this is a "Check-up" page to see what they have learned during the week. [**Note:** Teachers/parents of home schoolers may decide what will be assessed. If a student does exceptionally well on the "What do you know?" pre-assessment, the teacher may choose not to test words already known by the student. Or the teacher may choose to test all words for the week.]

2. Tell the students that you will say a word and use it in a sentence. They will listen to the word and the sentence. Then they will write the word on the line next to the numbers. All working words are included in this review.

3. Say the word. Repeat it in the context of a sentence. Repeat the word.

4. The students write the word dictated.

5. The process is repeated until all words have been tested.

6. The teacher may correct in class by writing the words on the board and having the students compare or "self-correct" their work. Or the teacher may correct each student's work individually.

7. The teacher then writes any corrections for words misspelled in the space provided.

8. The students study the misspelled words, then practice them on the second side of the Lesson page.

9. Space is provided for retesting, for testing additional sight or "working words" added for the week, and for additional practice.

Check-up Time! Lesson 85 Name:

Spelling Test

1.   11.
2.   12.
3.   13.
4.   14.
5.   15.
6.   16.
7.   17.
8.   18.
9.   19.
10.   20.

Corrections

Horizons Spelling Grade 2 141

Extended Activity:

Review any words missed. Send words to review home for additional study. Praise all efforts.

Week 18

Lessons 86-90 - Assess Student's Knowledge

Goal: To recognize the different spelling of the **er** sound in words (**er, ir, ur, wor, ear**).

Review Rule: An **r** after a vowel makes the vowel sound different from a short or long sound. Examples: **her, clerk, letter, first, dirt, nurse, fur, burn, work, early.**

What Do You Know?

Give the students the What do you know? page for Lessons 86-90. Tell them that this page will be used to see what they already know about the words for the week. Ask them to listen carefully to each word as you say it, repeat it in a sentence, and say it once again. Follow the procedures for this page as described in the *Introduction* at the beginning of this Teacher's Guide.

Show the children how to write their working words in the appropriate section at the back of their *Spelling Dictionary*.

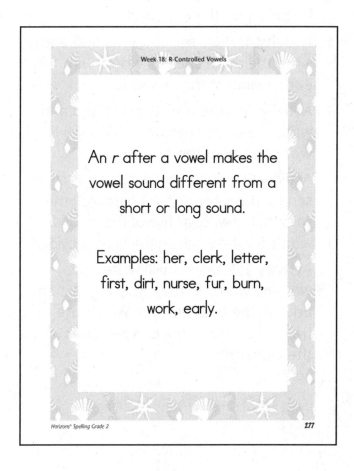

What do you know? Lessons 86-90	Name:	
Words for the Week	**Corrections**	**Practice**
1. nerve		1.
2. verb		2.
3. verse		3.
4. curb		4.
5. fur		5.
6. purse		6.
7. dirt		7.
8. sir		8.
9. stir		9.
10. early		10.
11. earth		11.
12. learn		12.
13. world		13.
14. work		14.
15. word		15.
16. below		16.
17. inside		17.

Horizons Spelling Grade 2   143

Week 18: R-Controlled Vowels

An *r* after a vowel makes the vowel sound different from a short or long sound.

Examples: her, clerk, letter, first, dirt, nurse, fur, burn, work, early.

Horizons® Spelling Grade 2   177

Lesson 86 - Introduce Words

Activities:

1. Give the students Lesson 86.

2. Put five columns on the board: **-er**, **-ir**, **-ur**, **wor**, and **ear**. These represent the five different spellings in English for the -er sound. Begin listing words for each column with the students' help (**her**, **first**, **nurse**, **word**, **early**).

3. **Activity 1:** Have the students find and write the three spelling words with the **er** spelling of the **er** sound.

4. **Activity 2:** Have the students find and write the three spelling words with the **ur** spelling of the **er** sound.

5. **Activity 3:** Have the students find and write the three spelling words with the **ir** spelling of the **er** sound.

6. **Activity 4:** Have the students find and write the three spelling words with the **ear** spelling of the **er** sound.

7. **Activity 5:** Have the students find and write the three spelling words with the **wor** spelling of the **er** sound.

8. **Activity 6:** Write the working words chosen for the week on the board. Ask the students to write all five of their working words for the week on the lines provided.

9. **Activity 7:** Students will write their working words in their Spelling dictionaries in the back section. Words are to be written under the correct letter of the alphabet.

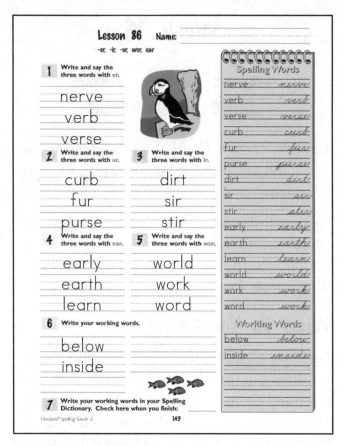

Extended Activities for the Week:

1. Send a list of the week's words home for further study. Emphasize the importance of using spelling words in sentences, in speech, in stories, etc., so that they are given a context and not simply memorized in isolation.

2. Assign reproducible *Week 18 Worksheet* either as homework or as an added classroom activity.

3. Have students write the definitions of the "choice" working words in their notebooks.

4. Have the students begin the writing of sentences for each spelling word in their notebooks.

5. Bring out or begin individual word family charts for each of the different spellings of the er sound.

Lesson 87 - Examine and Explore Words

Activities:

1. Give the students Lesson 87.

2. **Crossword Activity:** Have the students read the clue sentences and find and write the spelling word that completes the sentence. Check to make sure the students understand the crossword format.

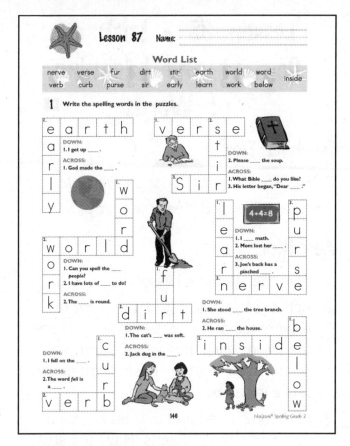

Extended Activities:

1. If students have visual difficulties with these crossword puzzles, provide additional practice with SINGLE puzzles. Cut the puzzles out so that they can focus on just one at a time.

2. Have the students continue the writing of sentences for each spelling word in their notebooks.

Lesson 88 - Look at Context and Meaning of Words

Teaching Tips:

1. Have Spelling dictionaries available.
2. Have Bible or Bible verse ready.

Activities:

1. Give the students Lesson 88.
2. **Activity 1:** Ask the students to write a sentence or sentences which include the words given in each of the three sections. Have them illustrate their sentence in the box provided.
3. **Activity 2:** Read and discuss the Bible verse with the students. Have the students write the verse, learn it from memory, and share it with a friend.

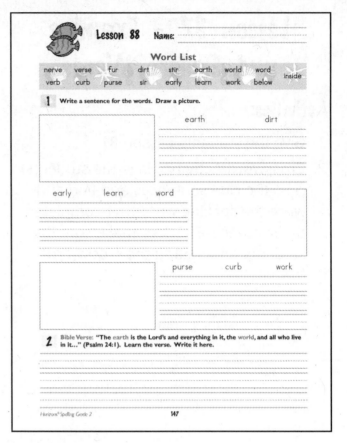

Extended Activities:

1. Share pictures and sentences from activity
2. Illustrate the Bible verse and share ideas.
3. Have the students continue the writing of sentences for each spelling word in their notebooks.

Lesson 89 - Apply Understanding of Words in Writing

Teaching Tips:

1. Have Spelling dictionaries available.
2. Have Bible stories of Creation available to read. Have picture Bibles available, if possible.

Activities:

1. Give the students Lesson 89.
2. **Writing Activity:** Read the Creation story to the students. Talk about it in light of the Bible verse for the week. Ask the students to write and illustrate their own summary of the Creation story. They may want to take their favorite day of Creation and use that.

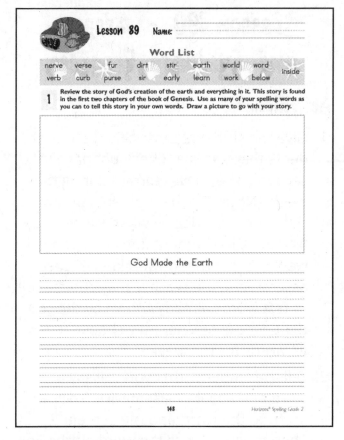

Extended Activities:

1. Share stories and pictures.
2. Have the students complete the writing of sentences for each spelling word in their notebooks.

Lesson 90 - Assess and Evaluate Progress

Activities:

1. Give the students Lesson 90. Tell the students that this is a "Check-up" page to see what they have learned during the week. [**Note:** Teachers/parents of home schoolers may decide what will be assessed. If a student does exceptionally well on the "What do you know?" pre-assessment, the teacher may choose not to test words already known by the student. Or the teacher may choose to test all words for the week.]

2. Tell the students that you will say a word and use it in a sentence. They will listen to the word and the sentence. Then they will write the word on the line next to the numbers. All working words are included in this review.

3. Say the word. Repeat it in the context of a sentence. Repeat the word.

4. The students write the word dictated.

5. The process is repeated until all words have been tested.

6. The teacher may correct in class by writing the words on the board and having the students compare or "self-correct" their work. Or the teacher may correct each student's work individually.

7. The teacher then writes any corrections for words misspelled in the space provided.

8. The students study the misspelled words, then practice them on the second side of the Lesson page.

9. Space is provided for retesting, for testing additional sight or "working words" added for the week, and for additional practice.

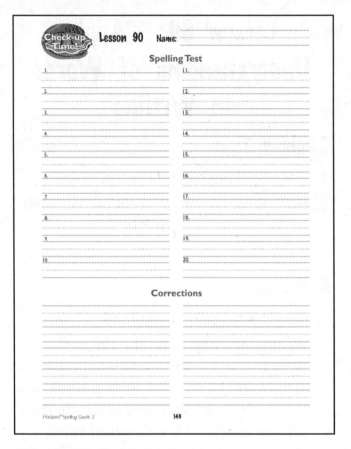

Extended Activity:

Review any words missed. Send words to review home for additional study. Praise all efforts.

Week 19

Lessons 91-95 - Assess Student's Knowledge

Goal: To recognize and spell words with **s** blends.

Review Rule: In an **s** blend, two or more consonants come together in word. Their sounds blend together, but each sound is heard. Examples: spell, snail.

What Do You Know?

Give the students the What do you know? page for Lessons 91-95. Tell them that this page will be used to see what they already know about the words for the week. Ask them to listen carefully to each word as you say it, repeat it in a sentence, and say it once again. Follow the procedures for this page as described in the *Introduction* at the beginning of this Teacher's Guide.

Show the children how to write their working words in the appropriate section at the back of their *Spelling Dictionary*.

In an *s* blend, two or more consonants come together in a word. Their sounds blend together, but each sound is heard.

Examples: spell, snail

Lesson 91 - Introduce Words

Activities:

1. Give the students Lesson 91.

2. Review **s** blends. Remind the students that they can come at the beginning, in the middle, or at the end of a word.

3. **Activity 1:** Have the students find and write the spelling word that has an **s** blend at both the beginning and the end of the word.

4. **Activity 2:** Have the students find and write the spelling words that begin with an **s** blend. They will NOT repeat the word from the first activity.

5. **Activity 3:** Have the students find and write the spelling words that end with an **s** blend. They will NOT repeat the word from the first activity.

6. **Activity 4:** Write the working words chosen for the week on the board. Ask the students to write all five of their working words for the week on the lines provided.

7. **Activity 5:** Students will write their working words in their Spelling dictionaries in the back section. Words are to be written under the correct letter of the alphabet.

Extended Activities for the Week:

1. Send a list of the week's words home for further study. Emphasize the importance of using spelling words in sentences, in speech, in stories, etc., so that they are given a context and not simply memorized in isolation.

2. Assign reproducible *Week 19 Worksheet* either as homework or as an added classroom activity.

3. Have students write the definitions of the "choice" working words in their notebooks.

4. Have the students begin the writing of sentences for each spelling word in their notebooks.

5. Bring out or begin individual word family charts for **s** blends.

Lesson 92 - Examine and Explore Words

Activities:

1. Give the students Lesson 92.

2. **Activity 1:** Review sorting of words in ABC order. Have the students arrange each group of words in order. Remind them to look to the third or fourth letter if needed.

3. **Activity 2:** Have the student find and write the four two-syllable spelling words. Have them draw a line between syllables. Have them circle the two-syllable word that is also a compound word.

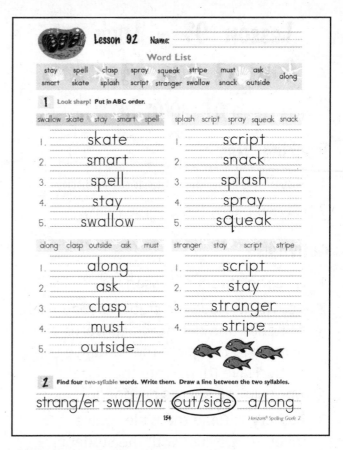

Extended Activities:

1. Give additional practice with ABC order as needed.

2. Have the students continue the writing of sentences for each spelling word in their notebooks.

Lesson 93 - Look at Context and Meaning of Words

Teaching Tips:

1. Have Spelling dictionaries available.
2. Have Bible or Bible verse ready.

Activities:

1. Give the students Lesson 93.
2. **Activity 1:** Have the students read each sentence and decide which words are needed to complete the sentence correctly. Have them write the correct words in the spaces provided.
3. **Activity 2:** Read the Bible verses together. Discuss with the students. What sorts of things are appropriate to ask for? Have the students write about things they would ask in Jesus name.

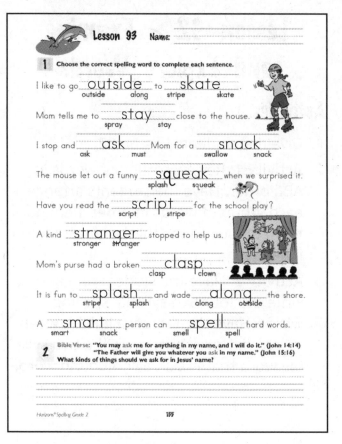

Extended Activities:

1. Share responses to the Bible verse question.
2. Have the students continue the writing of sentences for each spelling word in their notebooks.

Lesson 94 - Apply Understanding of Words in Writing

Teaching Tip:

Have Spelling dictionaries available.

Activities:

1. Give the students Lesson 94.
2. **Activity 1:** Ask the students to select two of their CHOICE working words to use in a sentence.
3. **Activity 2:** Ask the students to take the two words they chose from the first activity and write a definition for each.
4. **Activity 3:** Talk about snacks. Ask the students to draw a picture of their favorite snack. Write about it.

Lesson 94   Name: _____

Word List

stay	spell	clasp	spray	squeak	stripe	must	ask	along
smart	skate	splash	script	stranger	swallow	snack	outside	

1 Write a sentence for two of your working words.

2 Write a definition for two of your working words.

3 Write a story about your favorite snack. Draw a picture to go along with your story.

My Favorite Snack

156   Horizons Spelling Grade 2

Extended Activities:

1. Share definitions written by the students for the working words.
2. Share snack stories and pictures.
3. Have the students complete the writing of sentences for each spelling word in their notebooks.

Lesson 95 - Assess and Evaluate Progress

Activities:

1. Give the students Lesson 95. Tell the students that this is a "Check-up" page to see what they have learned during the week. [**Note:** Teachers/parents of home schoolers may decide what will be assessed. If a student does exceptionally well on the "What do you know?" pre-assessment, the teacher may choose not to test words already known by the student. Or the teacher may choose to test all words for the week.]

2. Tell the students that you will say a word and use it in a sentence. They will listen to the word and the sentence. Then they will write the word on the line next to the numbers. All working words are included in this review.

3. Say the word. Repeat it in the context of a sentence. Repeat the word.

4. The students write the word dictated.

5. The process is repeated until all words have been tested.

6. The teacher may correct in class by writing the words on the board and having the students compare or "self-correct" their work. Or the teacher may correct each student's work individually.

7. The teacher then writes any corrections for words misspelled in the space provided.

8. The students study the misspelled words, then practice them on the second side of the Lesson page.

9. Space is provided for retesting, for testing additional sight or "working words" added for the week, and for additional practice.

Extended Activity:

Review any words missed. Send words to review home for additional study. Praise all efforts.

Week 20

Lessons 96-100 - Assess Student's Knowledge

Goal: To recognize and spell homophones.

Review Rule: Homophones are words that sound alike but have different spellings and different meanings.

What Do You Know?

Give the students the What do you know? page for Lessons 96-100. Tell them that this page will be used to see what they already know about the words for the week. Ask them to listen carefully to each word as you say it, repeat it in a sentence, and say it once again. Follow the procedures for this page as described in the *Introduction* at the beginning of this Teacher's Guide.

Show the children how to write their working words in the appropriate section at the back of their *Spelling Dictionary*.

What do you know?
Lessons 96-100 Name:

Words for the Week	Corrections	Practice
bear		1.
bare		2.
tail		3.
tale		4.
hear		5.
here		6.
knows		7.
nose		8.
aunt		9.
ant		10.
read		11.
reed		12.
hour		13.
deer		14.
dear		15.
February		16.
valentine		17.

Horizons Spelling Grade 2   159

Week 20: Homophones

Homophones are words that sound alike but have different spellings and different meanings.

Examples: knows–nose, read–reed, bear–bare

Horizons® Spelling Grade 2   279

Lesson 96 - Introduce Words

Activities:

1. Give the students Lesson 96.

2. Review homophones. Write the word on the board. Begin with the homophones the students learned in Spelling 1: **to**, **two**; **weak**, **week**; **meet**, **meat**; **peek**, **peak**; **road**, **rode**; **ate**, **eight**. Write these on the board. Ask the students to add to the list.

3. **Activity 1:** Ask the students to identify each of the pictures. Have the students find and write the correct spelling for the homophone that belongs with the picture. Check to make sure they have done this correctly before having them write the homophone on the second line.

4. **Activity 2:** Write the working words chosen for the week on the board. Ask the students to write all five of their working words for the week on the lines provided.

5. **Activity 3:** Students will write their working words in their Spelling dictionaries in the back section. Words are to be written under the correct letter of the alphabet.

Extended Activities for the Week:

1. Send a list of the week's words home for further study. Emphasize the importance of using spelling words in sentences, in speech, in stories, etc., so that they are given a context and not simply memorized in isolation.

2. Assign reproducible *Week 20 Worksheet* either as homework or as an added classroom activity.

3. Have students write the definitions of the "choice" working words in their notebooks.

4. Have the students begin the writing of sentences for each spelling word in their notebooks.

5. Bring out or begin word family charts for homophones.

Lesson 97 – Examine and Explore Words

Teaching Tip:

Have Spelling dictionaries available.

Activities:

1. Give the students Lesson 97.

2. **Activity 1:** Have the students find and write the spelling word with three syllables.

3. **Activity 2:** Have the students find and write the spelling word with four syllables. Check to make sure they included the capital letter. Ask them why this word needs to begin with a capital letter [name of a month].

4. **Activity 3:** Ask the students to write a sentence using both words (valentine, February). Check for capital letters and correct sentence formation.

5. **Activity 4:** Tell the students that each sentence contains a spelling/meaning error. Have them find the error, circle it, and write the correct spelling on the line. [**Note:** Help students with visual discrimination problems.]

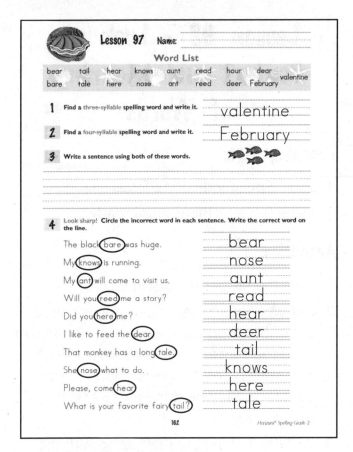

Extended Activities:

1. Make sets of homophone cards for the learning center. Make picture cards for those words that can be pictured. Use both sets of cards for drill and additional practice.

2. Have the students continue the writing of sentences for each spelling word in their notebooks.

Lesson 98 - Look at Context and Meaning of Words

Teaching Tips:

1. Have Spelling dictionaries available.
2. Have Bible or Bible verse ready.

Activities:

1. Give the students Lesson 98.
2. **Activity 1:** Each set of sentences uses a set of homophones. Ask the students to read the sentences and to write the correct spelling of the homophone in the sentence. May be done as a class or individually.
3. **Activity 2:** Read the Bible verse with the students and discuss it. How do they practice God's Word? Who teaches them about God's Word? Ask the students to write the verse on their own paper.

Extended Activities:

1. Have the students draw and write about at least one way they can put God's word into practice.
2. Have the students continue the writing of sentences for each spelling word in their notebooks.

Lesson 99 - Apply Understanding of Words in Writing

Teaching Tips:

1. Have Spelling dictionaries available.
2. Have different types of valentines available.

Activities:

1. Give the students Lesson 99.
2. **Writing Activity:** Talk about Valentine's Day. What do people do? Why do they do special things? What kind of special things do they do? (send flowers, give cards and gifts, etc.) Ask the students to design and write three different valentines: one for their families, one for their best friend, and one for God.

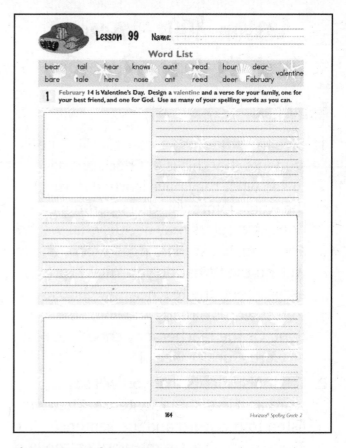

Extended Activities:

1. Share valentines.
2. Have the students complete the writing of sentences for each spelling word in their notebooks.

Lesson 100 - Assess and Evaluate Progress

Activities:

1. Give the students Lesson 100. Tell the students that this is a "Check-up" page to see what they have learned during the week. [**Note:** Teachers/parents of home schoolers may decide what will be assessed. If a student does exceptionally well on the "What do you know?" pre-assessment, the teacher may choose not to test words already known by the student. Or the teacher may choose to test all words for the week.]

2. Tell the students that you will say a word and use it in a sentence. They will listen to the word and the sentence. Then they will write the word on the line next to the numbers. All working words are included in this review.

3. Say the word. Repeat it in the context of a sentence. Repeat the word.

4. The students write the word dictated.

5. The process is repeated until all words have been tested.

6. The teacher may correct in class by writing the words on the board and having the students compare or "self-correct" their work. Or the teacher may correct each student's work individually.

7. The teacher then writes any corrections for words misspelled in the space provided.

8. The students study the misspelled words, then practice them on the second side of the Lesson page.

9. Space is provided for retesting, for testing additional sight or "working words" added for the week, and for additional practice.

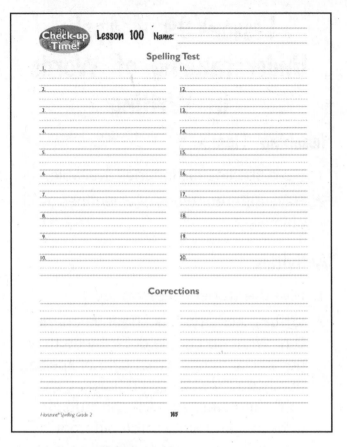

Check-up Time! Lesson 100 Name:

Spelling Test

1.
2.
3.
4.
5.
6.
7.
8.
9.
10.
11.
12.
13.
14.
15.
16.
17.
18.
19.
20.

Corrections

Horizons® Spelling Grade 2   185

Extended Activity:

Review any words missed. Send words to review home for additional study. Praise all efforts.

Week 21

Lessons 101-105 - Assess Student's Knowledge

Goal: To recognize and spell words with the **k** sound of **qu** and **ch**. To recognize and spell words with the **f** sound of **ph** and **gh**.

Review Rules:

The letters **qu** stand for the **kw** sound.

The letters **ph** and **gh** can stand for the **f** sound. Examples: **laugh**, **rough**, **tough**, **phone**, **elephant**.

What Do You Know?

Give the students the What do you know? page for Lessons 101-105. Tell them that this page will be used to see what they already know about the words for the week. Ask them to listen carefully to each word as you say it, repeat it in a sentence, and say it once again. Follow the procedures for this page as described in the *Introduction* at the beginning of this Teacher's Guide.

Show the children how to write their working words in the appropriate section at the back of their *Spelling Dictionary*.

What do you know? Lessons 101-105   Name: _____

Words for the Week	Corrections	Practice
1. quilt	1.	1.
2. quiet	2.	2.
3. quest	3.	3.
4. quietly	4.	4.
5. quiz	5.	5.
6. Christian	6.	6.
7. ache	7.	7.
8. tougher	8.	8.
9. roughly	9.	9.
10. toughest	10.	10.
11. alphabet	11.	11.
12. phonics	12.	12.
13. photograph	13.	13.
14. gopher	14.	14.
15. elephant	15.	15.
16. break	16.	16.
17. breakfast	17.	17.

Horizons Spelling Grade 2   167

Week 21: Consonant Digraphs ph and gh

The letters *ph* and *gh* can stand for the *f* sound.

Examples: laugh, rough, phone, elephant

Horizons® Spelling Grade 2   281

Lesson 101 - Introduce Words

Activities:

1. Give the students Lesson 101.

2. Make four columns on the board: **qu = kw**; **ch = k**; **ph = f**; **gh = f**. Ask the students to help you list words for each column.

3. **Activity 1:** Have the students complete the story by using the **qu** spelling words.

4. **Activity 2:** Have the students find and write the two spelling words in which the **ch** makes the **k** sound.

5. **Activity 3:** Have the students write the two working words given with the lesson in the correct shapes. Have them circle the word that is a compound word.

6. **Activity 4:** Write the working words chosen for the week on the board. Ask the students to write all five of their working words for the week on the lines provided.

7. **Activity 5:** Students will write their working words in their Spelling dictionaries in the back section. Words are to be written under the correct letter of the alphabet.

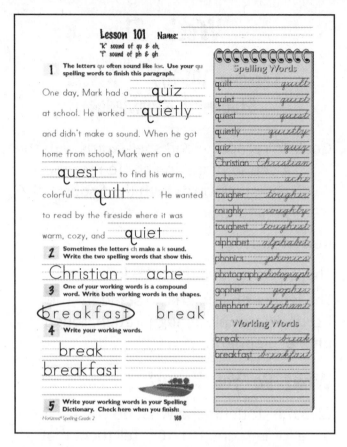

Extended Activities for the Week:

1. Send a list of the week's words home for further study. Emphasize the importance of using spelling words in sentences, in speech, in stories, etc., so that they are given a context and not simply memorized in isolation.

2. Assign reproducible *Week 21 Worksheet* either as homework or as an added classroom activity.

3. Have students write the definitions of the "choice" working words in their notebooks.

4. Have the students begin the writing of sentences for each spelling word in their notebooks.

5. Bring out or begin individual word family charts for the **qu (kw)** sound and the **ph** and **gh** spelling of the **f** sound.

Lesson 102 - Examine and Explore Words

Activities:

1. Give the students Lesson 102.

2. **Activity 1:** Have the students find and write the five spelling words in which the **f** sound is spelled with the consonant digraph **ph**. After they have written the words, have them draw shape boxes around each word. Have them circle the **ph**.

3. **Activity 2:** Have the students find and write the three spelling words in which the **f** sound is spelled with the consonant digraph **gh**. After they have written the words, have them draw shape boxes around each word. Have them circle the **gh**.

4. **Activity 3:** Have the students find and write the spelling words in the correct columns according to the number of syllables in each word.

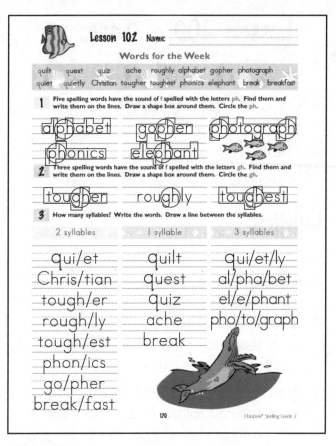

Extended Activities:

1. Build additional words using the **ph** and **gh** spelling of the **f** sound.

2. Build additional words using the **ph** and **gh** spelling of the **f** sound.

3. Have the students continue the writing of sentences for each spelling word in their notebooks.

Lesson 103 - Look at Context and Meaning of Words

Teaching Tip:

Have Spelling dictionaries available.

Activities:

1. Give the students Lesson 103.

2. **Activity 1:** The students will be writing five sentences in this activity. Ask them to look at the three words given for each sentence. Have them use the words in an original sentence.

3. **Activity 2:** Discuss ways in which the students can follow Christ. Have them write one of the ways in the space provided to complete the sentence.

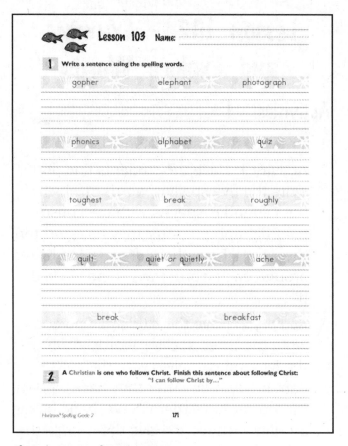

Extended Activities:

1. Share the sentences written in the first activity.

2. Share the ideas on following Christ.

3. Have the students continue the writing of sentences for each spelling word in their notebooks.

Lesson 104 - Apply Understanding of Words in Writing

Teaching Tips:

1. Have Spelling dictionaries available.

2. Have pictures of quilts available.

Activities:

1. Give the students Lesson 104.

2. **Writing Activity:** Begin by drawing a quilt of blank squares on the board. Ask the students how they would complete the quilt. What design or theme would they take for the squares? Have the students draw their own quilts in the space provided. Ask them to write a sentence that describes their quilt.

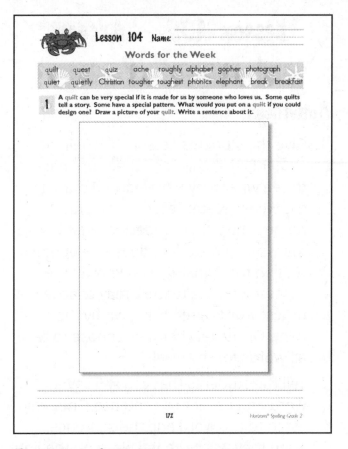

Extended Activities:

1. Share quilt ideas. Make a class bulletin board quilt in which each student designs one square.

2. Have the students complete the writing of sentences for each spelling word in their notebooks.

Lesson 105 - Assess and Evaluate Progress

Activities:

1. Give the students Lesson 105. Tell the students that this is a "Check-up" page to see what they have learned during the week. [**Note:** Teachers/parents of home schoolers may decide what will be assessed. If a student does exceptionally well on the "What do you know?" pre-assessment, the teacher may choose not to test words already known by the student. Or the teacher may choose to test all words for the week.]

2. Tell the students that you will say a word and use it in a sentence. They will listen to the word and the sentence. Then they will write the word on the line next to the numbers. All working words are included in this review.

3. Say the word. Repeat it in the context of a sentence. Repeat the word.

4. The students write the word dictated.

5. The process is repeated until all words have been tested.

6. The teacher may correct in class by writing the words on the board and having the students compare or "self-correct" their work. Or the teacher may correct each student's work individually.

7. The teacher then writes any corrections for words misspelled in the space provided.

8. The students study the misspelled words, then practice them on the second side of the Lesson page.

9. Space is provided for retesting, for testing additional sight or "working words" added for the week, and for additional practice.

Check-up Time! Lesson 105 Name: _____

Spelling Test

1.	11.
2.	12.
3.	13.
4.	14.
5.	15.
6.	16.
7.	17.
8.	18.
9.	19.
10.	20.

Corrections

Horizons Spelling Grade 2   173

Extended Activity:

Review any words missed. Send words to review home for additional study. Praise all efforts.

Week 22

Lessons 106-110 - Assess Student's Knowledge

Goal: To recognize and spell words with silent letters **gn**, **kn**, and **sc**. To recognize and spell the **z** sound of **s**.

Review Rules:

The consonant digraphs **gn** and **kn** stands for the **n** sound. The **g** and **k** are silent. Examples: **sign**, **gnaw**, **knife**

In the consonant digraph **sc** sometimes stand for the **s** sound.

The **c** is silent. Examples: **science**, **scent**.

Guide words appear at the top of each dictionary page. They tell what the first and last words on the page are.

What Do You Know?

Give the students the What do you know? page for Lessons 106-110. Tell them that this page will be used to see what they already know about the words for the week. Ask them to listen carefully to each word as you say it, repeat it in a sentence, and say it once again. Follow the procedures for this page as described in the *Introduction* at the beginning of this Teacher's Guide.

Show the children how to write their working words in the appropriate section at the back of their *Spelling Dictionary*.

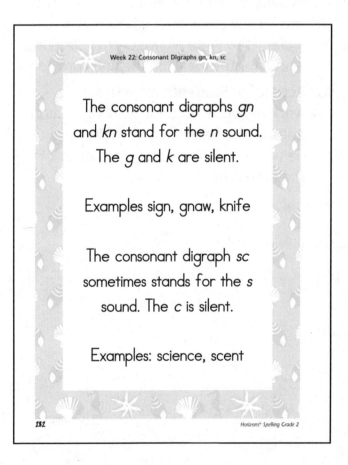

Lesson 106 - Introduce Words

Activities:

1. Give the students Lesson 106.

2. Review silent letter words.

3. **Activity 1:** Have the students find and write the spelling words in which the **s** has the same sound as a **z**.

4. **Activity 2:** Have the students find and write the two spelling words that are homophones (**needs, kneads**).

5. **Activity 3:** Have the students find and write the six spelling words that have a silent **k**.

6. **Activity 4:** Have the students find and write the three spelling words that have a silent **g**.

7. **Activity 5:** Write the working words chosen for the week on the board. Ask the students to write all five of their working words for the week on the lines provided.

8. **Activity 6:** Students will write their working words in their Spelling dictionaries in the back section. Words are to be written under the correct letter of the alphabet.

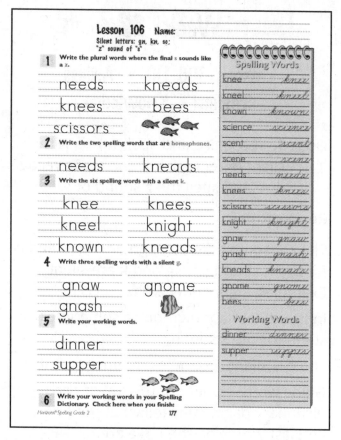

Extended Activities for the Week:

1. Send a list of the week's words home for further study. Emphasize the importance of using spelling words in sentences, in speech, in stories, etc., so that they are given a context and not simply memorized in isolation.

2. Assign reproducible *Week 22 Worksheet* either as homework or as an added classroom activity.

3. Have students write the definitions of the "choice" working words in their notebooks.

4. Have the students begin the writing of sentences for each spelling word in their notebooks.

5. Bring out or begin individual word family charts for each silent letter group.

Horizons Spelling Grade 2

Lesson 107 - Examine and Explore Words

Teaching Tip:

Have individual sets of the **kn** words for the students to use in the second activity.

Activities:

1. Give the students Lesson 107.

2. **Activity 1:** Have the students find and write the four spelling words that have a silent **c**.

3. **Activity 2:** Review ABC order. Have the students put the words in correct ABC order. Remind them that they may have to go to the fourth or fifth letter to find the correct order.

4. **Activity 3:** Have the students find and write the spelling words that match the definitions given.

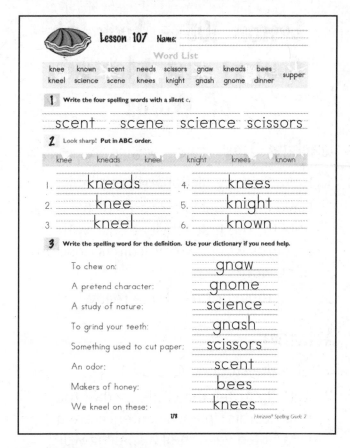

Extended Activities:

1. Have students look up and give definitions for the spelling words not used in the third activity.

2. Have the students continue the writing of sentences for each spelling word in their notebooks.

Lesson 108 - Look at Context and Meaning of Words

Teaching Tips:

1. Have Spelling dictionaries available.

2. Have individual letter cards or tiles available for the first activity to use with students who have difficulties unscrambling words.

3. Have Bible or Bible verse ready.

Activities:

1. Give the students Lesson 108.

2. **Activity 1:** Tell the students that the bold word(s) in each sentence are a scrambled version of a spelling word. Have them unscramble the words and write them correctly on the lines provided. [**Note:** Help students with visual discrimination problems.]

3. **Activity 2:** This is a new dictionary activity [**Note:** refer to rules, if desired]. Have the students take their Spelling dictionaries and open them to the first page of words. Have them look at the top of the page for the "guide words" for that page. Explain that the guide words give them a quick way of locating a word. Have them look up the word "**kneel**" in their dictionaries. What two guide words do they see at the top? Have them write the words. Repeat the process for the word "**scent**."

4. **Activity 3:** Read and pray the Bible verse with the students. Have them learn the verse, write it on their own paper, and share it with someone they love.

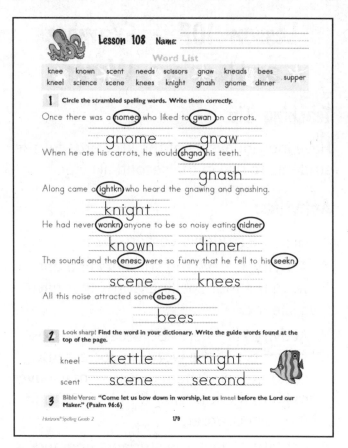

Extended Activities:

1. Give additional practice with guide words. See the Worksheet for this week. Have students find the guide words for words in previous units.

2. Have the students continue the writing of sentences for each spelling word in their notebooks.

Lesson 109 - Apply Understanding of Words in Writing

Teaching Tips:

1. Have Spelling dictionaries available.
2. Have books and pictures about knights and the Middle Ages available to spur discussion and ideas for story.

Activities:

1. Give the students Lesson 109.
2. **Writing Activity:** If any reference or story books are available that show knights and their life in the Middle Ages, have them out for the students to read and view. Ask them to think about what they would do if they could go back in time and be a knight for a day. Have them write their stories.

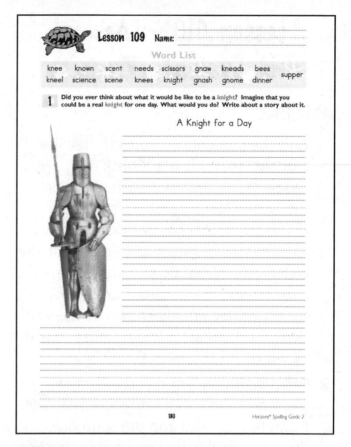

Extended Activities:

1. Share the stories and have the students illustrate them.
2. Have the students complete the writing of sentences for each spelling word in their notebooks.

Lesson 110 - Assess and Evaluate Progress

Activities:

1. Give the students Lesson 110. Tell the students that this is a "Check-up" page to see what they have learned during the week. [**Note:** Teachers/parents of home schoolers may decide what will be assessed. If a student does exceptionally well on the "What do you know?" pre-assessment, the teacher may choose not to test words already known by the student. Or the teacher may choose to test all words for the week.]

2. Tell the students that you will say a word and use it in a sentence. They will listen to the word and the sentence. Then they will write the word on the line next to the numbers. All working words are included in this review.

3. Say the word. Repeat it in the context of a sentence. Repeat the word.

4. The students write the word dictated.

5. The process is repeated until all words have been tested.

6. The teacher may correct in class by writing the words on the board and having the students compare or "self-correct" their work. Or the teacher may correct each student's work individually.

7. The teacher then writes any corrections for words misspelled in the space provided.

8. The students study the misspelled words, then practice them on the second side of the Lesson page.

9. Space is provided for retesting, for testing additional sight or "working words" added for the week, and for additional practice.

Extended Activity:

Review any words missed. Send words to review home for additional study. Praise all efforts.

Week 23

Lessons 111-115 - Assess Student's Knowledge

Goal: To recognize and spell comparative words ending in **-er** and **-est**.

Review Rules:

The suffix **-er** can be used to compare two things. Examples: **near/nearer**, **long/longer**. Sue is **shorter** than her sister (comparing two things).

The suffix **-est** is used to compare more than two things. Examples: **tall/tallest**, **short/shortest**. Sue is the **shortest** in her family (comparing more than two things).

When a word ends in **y** after a consonant, change the **y** to **i** before adding **er** to the end. Examples: **pretty/prettier**, **busy/busier**.

When a words ends in **y** after a consonant, change the **y** to **i** before adding **est** to the end. Examples: **pretty/prettiest**, **lonely/loneliest**.

If a word with a short vowel sound ends in a single consonant, usually double the consonant before adding a suffix that begins with a vowel. Examples: **big/bigger**, **biggest**; **fat/fatter**, **fattest**.

If a word ends in silent **e**, drop the **e** before adding a suffix that begins with a vowel. Examples: **write/writer**, **little/littler/littlest**.

What Do You Know?

Give the students the What do you know? page for Lessons 111-115. Tell them that this page will be used to see what they already know about the words for the week. Ask them to listen carefully to each word as you say it, repeat it in a sentence, and say it once again. Follow the procedures for this page as described in the *Introduction* at the beginning of this Teacher's Guide.

Show the children how to write their working words in the appropriate section at the back of their *Spelling Dictionary*.

What do you know?

Lessons 111-115   Name:

Words for the Week	Corrections	Practice
1. bigger		1.
2. biggest		2.
3. smaller		3.
4. smallest		4.
5. stronger		5.
6. strongest		6.
7. happier		7.
8. happiest		8.
9. better		9.
10. best		10.
11. thinner		11.
12. thinnest		12.
13. littler		13.
14. littlest		14.
15. prettiest		15.
16. March		16.
17. without		17.

Horizons Spelling Grade 2   189

Week 23: Comparisons Using Suffixes -er and -est

The suffix *-er* can be used to compare two things.

Examples: near-nearer, long-longer, short-shorter

The suffix *-est* is used to compare more than two things.

Examples: tall-tallest, short-shortest

154   *Horizons® Spelling Grade 2*

Lesson 111 - Introduce Words

Activities:

1. Give the students Lesson 111.

2. Review comparatives. Make three columns on the board. Write out a few comparisons to get the students started:

   > long/longer/longest
   > soft/softer/softest
   > kind/kinder/kindest
   > fast/faster/fastest

   Have the students add to the list. Include some irregular comparisons: **good, better, best.** Remind the students of the difference when they compare two things and use the **-er** ending and when they compare three or more things and use the **-est** ending.

3. **Activity 1:** Have the students find and write the spelling word that is both the name of a month and something that people do in a parade.

4. **Activity 2:** Have the students find and write the spelling word that is a compound word. Ask them to draw a line between the two words.

5. **Activity 3:** Have the students find and write the spelling words that complete the word puzzles given. NOTE the following: (1) the changing of **y** to **i** before adding the ending in **happier**; (2) the doubling of the consonant before adding the ending in **thinner, bigger**; (3) the dropping of the final **e** before adding the **er** in **littler.**

6. **Activity 4:** Write the working words chosen for the week on the board. Ask the students to write all five of their working words for the week on the lines provided.

7. **Activity 5:** Students will write their working words in their Spelling dictionaries in the back section. Words are to be written under the correct letter of the alphabet.

Extended Activities for the Week:

1. Send a list of the week's words home for further study. Emphasize the importance of using spelling words in sentences, in speech, in stories, etc., so that they are given a context and not simply memorized in isolation.

2. Assign reproducible *Week 23 Worksheet* either as homework or as an added classroom activity.

3. Have students write the definitions of the "choice" working words in their notebooks.

4. Have the students begin the writing of sentences for each spelling word in their notebooks.

5. Bring out or begin individual word family charts for comparatives.

Horizons Spelling Grade 2

Lesson 112 - Examine and Explore Words

Teaching Tips:

1. Review rules for the week.
2. Review irregular comparisons: **good, better, best; some, more, most.**

Activities:

1. Give the students Lesson 112.
2. **Activity 1:** Have the students find and write the spelling words that complete the word puzzles given. NOTE spelling changes as in previous lesson.
3. **Activity 2:** Call attention to the irregular comparison. Have the students trace the words.
4. **Activity 3:** Ask the students to read the sentence and then decide which word is needed to complete the sentence correctly. Have the students circle the correct word.

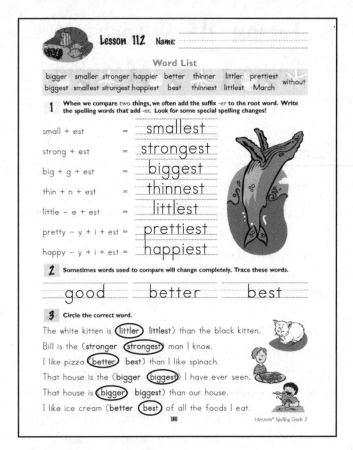

Extended Activities:

1. If students are having problems with comparatives, give additional practice. Make sets of picture/word cards to help them.
2. Have the students continue the writing of sentences for each spelling word in their notebooks.

Lesson 113 - Look at Context and Meaning of Words

Teaching Tips:

1. Have Bible and verse ready.
2. Have cards or markers available for students who need assistance finding the words in the puzzle.

Activities:

1. Give the students Lesson 113.
2. **Activity 1:** Have the students find and circle the spelling words in the word search puzzle. Word will be found moving both across and from top to bottom. Provide assistance for students with visual discrimination problems.
3. **Activity 2:** Read and discuss the Bible verse with the students. Remind them that this applies to everything they do at home, at play, in church, and at school. Have them stop and review the school day they are in. Have they given God their best in every subject? In every word they wrote? In every task they were asked to do? Have them write a sentence about how they can give their best efforts to God.

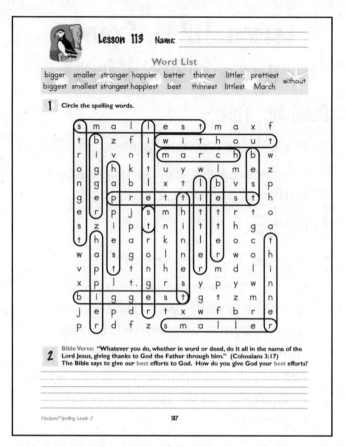

Extended Activities:

1. If students continue to have difficulties with words search puzzles, provide some very simple puzzles with LARGE letters and few words to help them.
2. Have the students continue the writing of sentences for each spelling word in their notebooks.

Lesson 114 - Apply Understanding of Words in Writing

Teaching Tip:

Have Spelling dictionaries available.

Activities:

1. Give the students Lesson 114.
2. **Writing Activity:** Have the students finish each sentence that has been started for them.

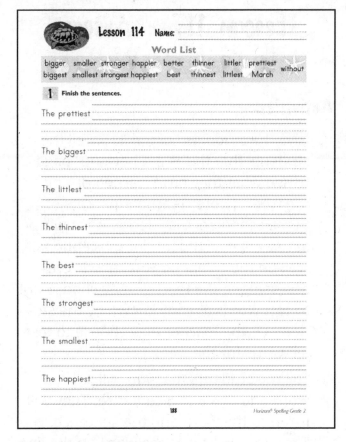

Extended Activities:

1. Share the sentences written. Have the students select two or three to illustrate.

2. Have the students complete the writing of sentences for each spelling word in their notebooks.

Lesson 115 - Assess and Evaluate Progress

Activities:

1. Give the students Lesson 115. Tell the students that this is a "Check-up" page to see what they have learned during the week. [**Note:** Teachers/parents of home schoolers may decide what will be assessed. If a student does exceptionally well on the "What do you know?" pre-assessment, the teacher may choose not to test words already known by the student. Or the teacher may choose to test all words for the week.]

2. Tell the students that you will say a word and use it in a sentence. They will listen to the word and the sentence. Then they will write the word on the line next to the numbers. All working words are included in this review.

3. Say the word. Repeat it in the context of a sentence. Repeat the word.

4. The students write the word dictated.

5. The process is repeated until all words have been tested.

6. The teacher may correct in class by writing the words on the board and having the students compare or "self-correct" their work. Or the teacher may correct each student's work individually.

7. The teacher then writes any corrections for words misspelled in the space provided.

8. The students study the misspelled words, then practice them on the second side of the Lesson page.

9. Space is provided for retesting, for testing additional sight or "working words" added for the week, and for additional practice.

Extended Activity:

Review any words missed. Send words to review home for additional study. Praise all efforts.

Week 24

Lessons 116-120 - Assess Student's Knowledge

Goal: To review spelling words from Lessons 81-115.

Review Rules: Review all rules used in the last seven weeks.

What Do You Remember?

Give the students the What do you remember? page for Lessons 81-115. Tell them that this page will be used to see what they remember about the words they have studied so far this year. Select an additional four to six Working Words from the list of words added each week. Ask them to listen carefully to each word as you say it, repeat it in a sentence, and say it once again. Follow the procedures for this page as described in the Introduction at the beginning of this Teacher's Guide.

(NOTE: If you have kept records of words that each child continues to find difficult, you may want to adjust the words in this unit to fit the needs of the individual child. Replace review words already mastered with those still needing work.)

Show the children how to write their working words in the appropriate section at the back of their *Spelling Dictionary*.

What do you remember? Lessons 81-115 Name: _____

Write the words your teacher reads.

1. how
2. slow
3. south
4. count
5. below
6. inside
7. early
8. world
9. along
10. must
11. ask
12. smart
13. hour
14. here
15. dear
16. hear
17. Christian
18. alphabet
19. Quiet
20. phonics
21. scissors
22. dinner
23. supper
24. known
25. without
26. best
27. better
28. biggest

Horizons Spelling Grade 2   181

Lesson 116 - Introduce Words

Activities:

1. Give the students Lesson 116.

2. **Activity 1:** Have the students find and write the thirteen two-syllable review spelling words. Provide any help necessary in word division.

3. **Activity 2:** Have the students find and write the three-syllable review word.

4. **Activity 3:** Have the students find and write the spelling word with a silent **k**.

5. **Activity 4:** Have the students find and write the homophone for each word given.

6. **Activity 5:** Select, or have the students select, five of the CHOICE working words to be reviewed in this unit. The words may be chosen for the class, or on an individual basis according to the needs of the student. Have the students write a sentence for each word.

Extended Activities for the Week:

1. Send a list of the week's words home for further study. Emphasize the importance of using spelling words in sentences, in speech, in stories, etc., so that they are given a context and not simply memorized in isolation.

2. Assign reproducible *Week 24 Worksheet* either as homework or as an added classroom activity.

3. Have students review the definitions of the "choice" working words in their notebooks.

4. Bring out individual word family charts for review.

Lesson 117 – Examine and Explore Words

Teaching Tips:

1. Have Spelling dictionaries available.
2. Have rule pages and word family charts available.

Activities:

1. Give the students Lesson 117.
2. **Activity 1:** Have the students find and write the six review spelling words with the **er** sound.
3. **Activity 2:** Have the students find and write the three compound review spelling words.
4. **Activity 3:** Have the students find and write the four review spelling words with the **ou** sound in **mouth**.
5. **Activity 4:** Have the students find and write the review spelling words that complete the two comparisons.
6. **Activity 5:** Have the students find and write the review spelling words for each **s** blend given.
7. **Activity 6:** Have the students find and write the review spelling word that begins with a capital letter. Have them use this word in an original sentence.

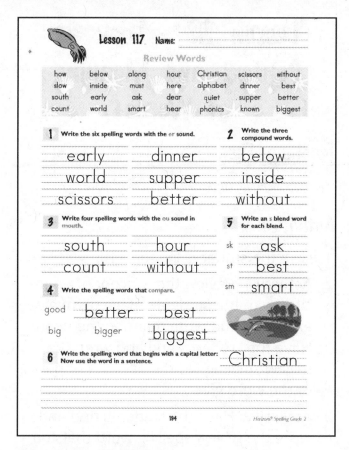

Extended Activities:

1. Note any areas where students are having difficulties and provide extra practice.
2. Review Bible stories and verses used in this review period.

Lesson 118 - Look at Context and Meaning of Words

Teaching Tip:

Have Spelling dictionaries available.

Activities:

1. Give the students Lesson 118.

2. **Activity 1:** Review the concept of opposites with the students. Have them give examples and write them on the board. Have the students find and write the review spelling word that is the opposite of the word given.

3. **Activity 2:** Have the students find and write the review spelling word that completes each sentence.

Extended Activities:

1. Give additional practice with opposites.

2. Continue individual help with areas of difficulty.

Lesson 119 - Apply Understanding of Words in Writing

Teaching Tips:

1. Have Spelling dictionaries available.
2. Have pictures of God's world available that show both the world "taken care of" and the world "misused."

Activities:

1. Give the students Lesson 119.
2. **Writing Activity:** Talk about ways to take care of the world God has given us. As a Christian, we have a duty to take care of all that God gave us. Recall the story of creation. God found all that he was made to be good. We must take care of all these "good" things God has given us. Have the students write and illustrate a story about ways in which they can take care of God's world.

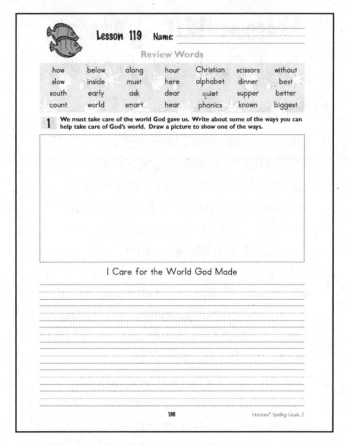

Extended Activity:

Share stories and pictures. Perhaps create a bulletin board of ways to take care of God's world.

Lesson 120 - Assess and Evaluate Progress

Activities:

1. Give the students Lesson120. Tell the students that this is a "Check-up" page to see what they have learned during the week. [**Note:** Teachers/parents of home schoolers may decide what will be assessed. If a student does exceptionally well on the "What do you know?" pre-assessment, the teacher may choose not to test words already known by the student. Or the teacher may choose to test all words for the week.]

2. Tell the students that you will say a word and use it in a sentence. They will listen to the word and the sentence. Then they will write the word on the line next to the numbers. All working words are included in this review.

3. Say the word. Repeat it in the context of a sentence. Repeat the word.

4. The students write the word dictated.

5. The process is repeated until all words have been tested.

6. The teacher may correct in class by writing the words on the board and having the students compare or "self-correct" their work. Or the teacher may correct each student's work individually.

7. The teacher then writes any corrections for words misspelled in the space provided.

8. The students study the misspelled words, then practice them on the second side of the Lesson page.

9. Space is provided for retesting, for testing additional sight or "working words" added for the week, and for additional practice.

Check-up Time! Lesson 120 Name: _____

Write the words your teacher reads.

1. _____   18. _____
2. _____   19. _____
3. _____   20. _____
4. _____   21. _____
5. _____   22. _____
6. _____   23. _____
7. _____   24. _____
8. _____   25. _____
9. _____   26. _____
10. _____   27. _____
11. _____   28. _____
12. _____
13. _____
14. _____
15. _____
16. _____
17. _____

Horizons Spelling Grade 2   197

Extended Activity:

Review any words missed. Send words to review home for additional study. Praise all efforts.

Week 25

Lessons 121-125 - Assess Student's Knowledge

Goal: To recognize and spell possessive form of words ending in **s** and **'s**. To recognize and spell the **k** sound of **ck**.

Review Rules:

In consonant digraph **ck** the **c** and the **k** go together to make the **k** sound. Examples: **clock**, **back**.

To make a singular noun show possession, add an apostrophe and an **s** (**'s**) at the end of the word. Examples: **boy's**, **child's**.

When a plural noun ends in **s**, usually add an apostrophe to show possession.

What Do You Know?

Give the students the What do you know? page for Lessons 121-125. Tell them that this page will be used to see what they already know about the words for the week. Ask them to listen carefully to each word as you say it, repeat it in a sentence, and say it once again. Follow the procedures for this page as described in the *Introduction* at the beginning of this Teacher's Guide.

Show the children how to write their working words in the appropriate section at the back of their *Spelling Dictionary*.

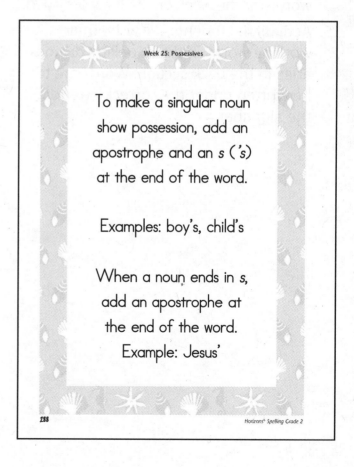

Lesson 121 - Introduce Words

Activities:

1. Give the students Lesson 121.

2. **Activity 1:** Review possessives. Ask the students to find a possessive spelling word to complete each of the descriptions. No word will be repeated. [**Note:** For the second and third examples, accept **either** *child's* or *girl's* as answers.]

3. **Activity 2:** Explain that possessive pronouns DO NOT use an apostrophe. Ask the students to find the three possessive pronouns and write them on the lines provided.

4. **Activity 3:** Write the working words chosen for the week on the board. Ask the students to write all five of their working words for the week on the lines provided.

5. **Activity 4:** Students will write their working words in their Spelling dictionaries in the back section. Words are to be written under the correct letter of the alphabet.

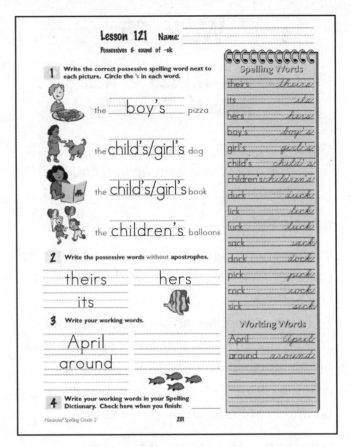

Extended Activities for the Week:

1. Send a list of the week's words home for further study. Emphasize the importance of using spelling words in sentences, in speech, in stories, etc., so that they are given a context and not simply memorized in isolation.

2. Assign reproducible *Week 25 Worksheet* either as homework or as an added classroom activity.

3. Have students write the definitions of the "choice" working words in their notebooks.

4. Have the students begin the writing of sentences for each spelling word in their notebooks.

5. Bring out or begin individual word family charts for possessives and for **-ck** words.

Lesson 122 - Examine and Explore Words

Activities:

1. Give the students Lesson 122.

2. **Activity 1:** Ask the students to read each sentence and to decide which of the words given is the correct possessive form. Ask them to circle the correct word and then write it on the line provided.

3. **Activity 2:** Remind the students that the ending -**ck** always has the sound of **k**. Ask the students to find and write the spelling words ending in -**ck** that rhyme with the words given.

4. **Activity 3:** Review ABC order. Ask the students to arrange the words in the correct ABC order.

5. **Activity 4:** Provide paper for the students to write sentences for each of their working words. Check sentences individually or have them read aloud in class as time permits.

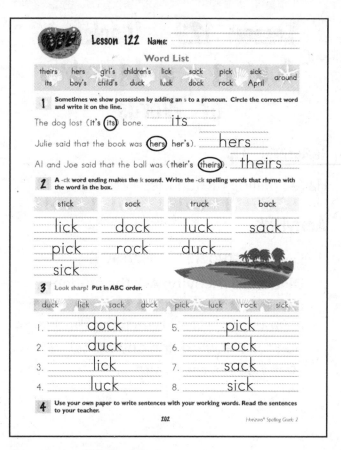

Extended Activities:

1. Have the students continue the writing of sentences for each spelling word in their notebooks.

2. Ask students to add to the -**ck** word family chart with other words they have learned.

Lesson 123 - Look at Context and Meaning of Words

Teaching Tip:

Have Spelling dictionaries available.

Activities:

1. Give the students Lesson 123.

2. **Dictionary Activity:** Ask the students to find each word given in their Spelling dictionaries. Have them write the definition for the word and an original sentence for each word.

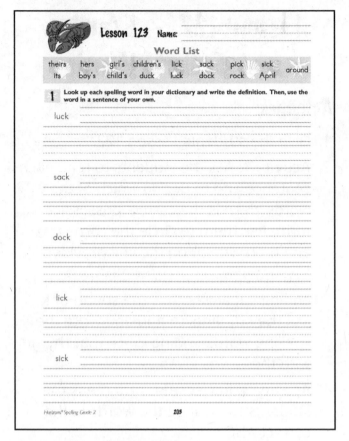

Extended Activities:

1. Share the sentences written.

2. Have the students continue the writing of sentences for each spelling word in their notebooks.

Lesson 124 - Apply Understanding of Words in Writing

Teaching Tips:

1. Have Spelling dictionaries available.
2. Have Bible story ready.

Activities:

1. Give the students Lesson 124.
2. **Writing Activity**: Read the Bible story and discuss Jesus' love for students. Ask the students to draw a picture of the story. Have them write about the story in their own words.

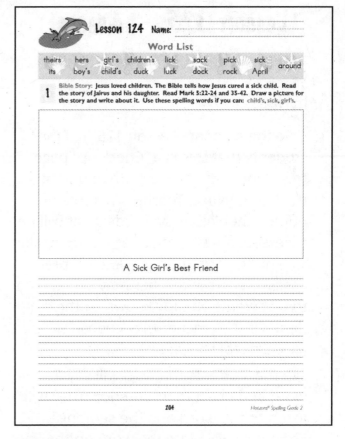

A Sick Girl's Best Friend

Extended Activities:

1. Share pictures and further discuss the story from the students' point of view.
2. Act out the story if time allows.
3. Have the students complete the writing of sentences for each spelling word in their notebooks.

Lesson 125 - Assess and Evaluate Progress

Activities:

1. Give the students Lesson 125. Tell the students that this is a "Check-up" page to see what they have learned during the week. [**Note:** Teachers/parents of home schoolers may decide what will be assessed. If a student does exceptionally well on the "What do you know?" pre-assessment, the teacher may choose not to test words already known by the student. Or the teacher may choose to test all words for the week.]

2. Tell the students that you will say a word and use it in a sentence. They will listen to the word and the sentence. Then they will write the word on the line next to the numbers. All working words are included in this review.

3. Say the word. Repeat it in the context of a sentence. Repeat the word.

4. The students write the word dictated.

5. The process is repeated until all words have been tested.

6. The teacher may correct in class by writing the words on the board and having the students compare or "self-correct" their work. Or the teacher may correct each student's work individually.

7. The teacher then writes any corrections for words misspelled in the space provided.

8. The students study the misspelled words, then practice them on the second side of the Lesson page.

9. Space is provided for retesting, for testing additional sight or "working words" added for the week, and for additional practice.

Extended Activity:

Review any words missed. Send words to review home for additional study. Praise all efforts.

Week 26

Lessons 126-130 - Assess Student's Knowledge

Goal: To recognize and spell words with l blends.

Review Rules:

In an l blend, two or more consonants come together in a word. Their sounds blend together, but each sound is heard. Examples: **black**, **plant**, **sled**.

Guide words appear at the top of each dictionary page. They tell what the first and last words on the page are.

What Do You Know?

Give the students the What do you know? page for Lessons 126-130. Tell them that this page will be used to see what they already know about the words for the week. Ask them to listen carefully to each word as you say it, repeat it in a sentence, and say it once again. Follow the procedures for this page as described in the *Introduction* at the beginning of this Teacher's Guide.

Show the children how to write their working words in the appropriate section at the back of their *Spelling Dictionary*.

What do you know?
Lessons 126-130   Name: _____

Words for the Week	Corrections	Practice
1. plate		1.
2. plan		2.
3. flake		3.
4. flame		4.
5. glue		5.
6. globe		6.
7. bluff		7.
8. blame		8.
9. click		9.
10. clothes		10.
11. please		11.
12. glad		12.
13. flower		13.
14. blend		14.
15. class		15.
16. became		16.
17. become		17.

Horizons Spelling Grade 2   207

Week 26: l Blends

In an l blend, two or more consonants come together in a word. Their sounds blend together, but each sound is heard.

Examples: black, plant, sled

Horizons Spelling Grade 2   239

Lesson 126 - Introduce Words

Activities:

1. Give the students Lesson 126.

2. Review l blends. Point out that the l will not be the first letter in the blend, but the second.

3. **Activity 1:** Have the students find and write the spelling words that begin with the **cl** blend.

4. **Activity 2:** Have the students find and write the spelling words that begin with the **bl** blend.

5. **Activity 3:** Have the students find and write the spelling words that begin with the **pl** blend.

6. **Activity 4:** Have the students find and write the spelling words that begin with the **fl** blend.

7. **Activity 5:** Have the students find and write the spelling words that begin with the **gl** blend.

8. **Activity 6:** Write the working words chosen for the week on the board. Ask the students to write all five of their working words for the week on the lines provided.

9. **Activity 7:** Students will write their working words in their Spelling dictionaries in the back section. Words are to be written under the correct letter of the alphabet.

Extended Activities for the Week:

1. Send a list of the week's words home for further study. Emphasize the importance of using spelling words in sentences, in speech, in stories, etc., so that they are given a context and not simply memorized in isolation.

2. Assign reproducible *Week 26 Worksheet* either as homework or as an added classroom activity.

3. Have students write the definitions of the "choice" working words in their notebooks.

4. Have the students begin the writing of sentences for each spelling word in their notebooks.

5. Bring out or begin individual word family charts for l blends.

Lesson 127 - Examine and Explore Words

Activities:

1. Give the students Lesson 127.

2. **Activity 1:** Have the students read the clues, select the correct spelling word from the list, and write it in the appropriate section of the puzzle.

3. **Activity 2:** Have the students write the words given in the correct ABC order. Remind them to look to the second and third letter if needed to determine the order.

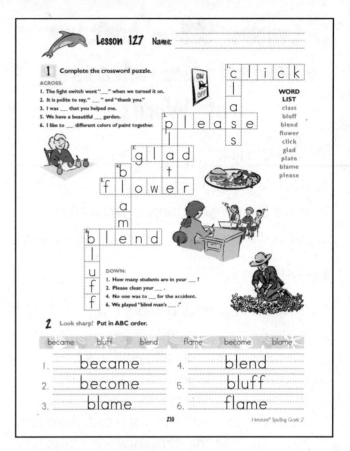

Extended Activities:

1. Give additional practice for ABC order as needed for this lesson and the next.

2. Have the students continue the writing of sentences for each spelling word in their notebooks.

Lesson 128 - Look at Context and Meaning of Words

Teaching Tips:

1. Review guide words.
2. Have Spelling dictionaries available.
3. Have Bible available for extended activity.

Activities:

1. Give the students Lesson 128.

2. **Activity 1:** Explain that each sentence contains a scrambled spelling word printed in bold print. Ask the students to find and write the correct spelling word for each scrambled word. Remind them to read the sentence for a clue to the correct word.

3. **Activity 2:** Have the students write the spelling words given in the correct ABC order. Remind them to look to the second or third letter if needed to determine the order.

4. **Activity 3:** Have the students find the words given in their Spelling dictionaries. Ask them to write the guide words from the top of the page on the lines provided.

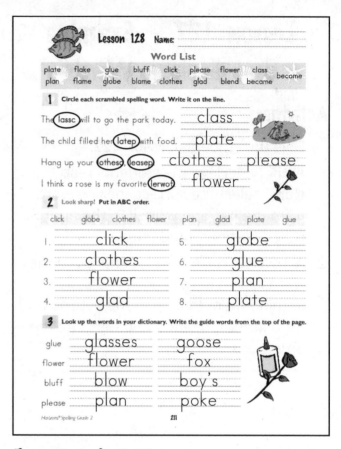

Extended Activities:

1. **Bible Activity:** "The angel of the Lord appeared to him [Moses] in flames of fire from within a bush." Read this section of Exodus 3 to the students. Talk about what Moses must have thought to see the bush in flames without being actually burnt. Have them write the verse and illustrate it.

2. Have the students continue the writing of sentences for each spelling word in their notebooks.

Lesson 129 - Apply Understanding of Words in Writing

Teaching Tip:

Have Spelling dictionaries available.

Activities:

1. Give the students Lesson 129.

2. **Writing Activity:** Brainstorm with the students about their favorite things. Have them choose one category: food, friends, stories, books, pets, etc. and write about their favorite thing in that category. Have them draw a picture for the story.

Lesson 129   Name: ....

Word List

plate	flake	glue	bluff	click*	please	flower	class	
plan	flame	globe	blame	clothes	glad	blend	become	become

1 Write a story about one of your favorite things (food, activity, class, book, pet, car, flower...or any other favorite you choose) and draw a picture to go with your story.

One of My Favorite Things Is...

111   Horizons® Spelling Grade 2

Extended Activities:

1. Share stories and pictures.

2. Have the students complete the writing of sentences for each spelling word in their notebooks.

Lesson 130 - Assess and Evaluate Progress

Activities:

1. Give the students Lesson 130. Tell the students that this is a "Check-up" page to see what they have learned during the week. [**Note:** Teachers/parents of home schoolers may decide what will be assessed. If a student does exceptionally well on the "What do you know?" pre-assessment, the teacher may choose not to test words already known by the student. Or the teacher may choose to test all words for the week.]

2. Tell the students that you will say a word and use it in a sentence. They will listen to the word and the sentence. Then they will write the word on the line next to the numbers. All working words are included in this review.

3. Say the word. Repeat it in the context of a sentence. Repeat the word.

4. The students write the word dictated.

5. The process is repeated until all words have been tested.

6. The teacher may correct in class by writing the words on the board and having the students compare or "self-correct" their work. Or the teacher may correct each student's work individually.

7. The teacher then writes any corrections for words misspelled in the space provided.

8. The students study the misspelled words, then practice them on the second side of the Lesson page.

9. Space is provided for retesting, for testing additional sight or "working words" added for the week, and for additional practice.

Extended Activity:

Review any words missed. Send words to review home for additional study. Praise all efforts.

Week 27

Lessons 131-135 - Assess Student's Knowledge

Goal: To recognize and spell irregular plurals. To recognize and spell words ending in **-x** and **-xes**.

Review Rules:

Some words form their plurals in an unusual way. Examples: **goose/geese**, **mouse/mice**.

For some words the singular and plural forms are the same. Example: **deer/deer**, **sheep/ sheep**.

If a word ends in **x**, **ch**, and **ss**, add the suffix **-es** to make the word plural.

What Do You Know?

Give the students the What do you know? page for Lessons 131-135. Tell them that this page will be used to see what they already know about the words for the week. Ask them to listen carefully to each word as you say it, repeat it in a sentence, and say it once again. Follow the procedures for this page as described in the *Introduction* at the beginning of this Teacher's Guide.

Show the children how to write their working words in the appropriate section at the back of their *Spelling Dictionary*.

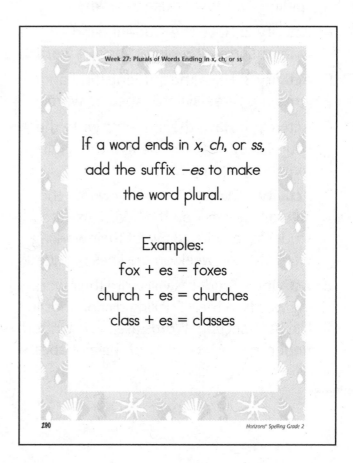

What do you know? Lessons 131-135 Name:

Words for the Week — Corrections — Practice

1. sheep
2. oxen
3. mice
4. geese
5. fox
6. mix
7. mixes
8. wax
9. waxes
10. ox
11. foxes
12. axes
13. books
14. churches
15. glasses
16. xylophone
17. across

Horizons Spelling Grade 2 — 215

Week 27: Plurals of Words Ending in x, ch, or ss

If a word ends in *x, ch,* or *ss,* add the suffix *−es* to make the word plural.

Examples:
fox + es = foxes
church + es = churches
class + es = classes

290 — *Horizons® Spelling Grade 2*

Lesson 131 - Introduce Words

Activities:

1. Give the students Lesson 131.

2. Review rule for plural of words ending in **x**. Write the words "Irregular Plurals" on the board. Explain to the students that irregular plurals are words that form the plural, not by adding **-s** or **-es**, but either by changing the singular word or keeping the singular form as the plural form. Demonstrate with the spelling words for this unit: **sheep/sheep; ox/oxen; mouse/mice; goose/geese**.

3. **Activity 1:** Review the rules for plurals of words ending in **s**, **x**, **ch**, or **sh**. Ask the students to find and write the plural spelling words that use **-s** or **-es**.

4. **Activity 2:** Have the students find and write the irregular plural spelling words.

5. **Activity 3:** Have the students find and write the three-syllable spelling word.

6. **Activity 4:** Have the students write the sound they hear for the **x** at the beginning of **xylophone**.

7. **Activity 5:** Write the working words chosen for the week on the board. Ask the students to write all five of their working words for the week on the lines provided.

8. **Activity 6:** Students will write their working words in their Spelling dictionaries in the back section. Words are to be written under the correct letter of the alphabet.

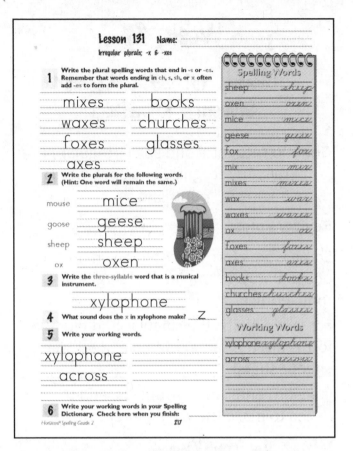

Extended Activities for the Week:

1. Send a list of the week's words home for further study. Emphasize the importance of using spelling words in sentences, in speech, in stories, etc., so that they are given a context and not simply memorized in isolation.

2. Assign reproducible *Week 27 Worksheet* either as homework or as an added classroom activity.

3. Have students write the definitions of the "choice" working words in their notebooks.

4. Have the students begin the writing of sentences for each spelling word in their notebooks.

5. Bring out or begin individual word family charts for irregular plurals.

Lesson 132 - Examine and Explore Words

Teaching Tip:

Have Spelling dictionaries available.

Activities:

1. Give the students Lesson 132.

2. **Activity 1:** Ask the students to find and write the plural spelling word needed to complete each sentence of the story.

3. **Activity 2:** Have the students read the definitions given and find and write the spelling word for each definition.

4. **Activity 3:** Have the students select two CHOICE working words and write them in a sentence. Check.

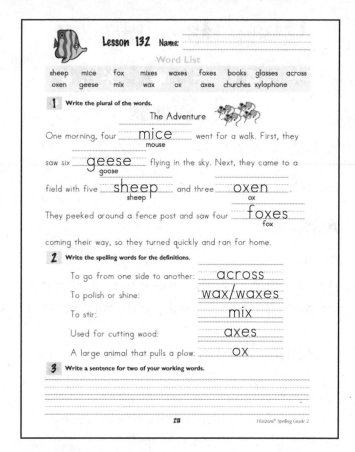

Extended Activities:

1. Make singular/plural card sets for all words that students know which have irregular plurals. Keep in learning center for additional practice.

2. Have the students continue the writing of sentences for each spelling word in their notebooks.

Lesson 133 - Look at Context and Meaning of Words

Teaching Tip:

Have Spelling dictionaries available.

Activities:

1. Give the students Lesson 133.

2. **Activity 1:** Ask the students to find and write the spelling word that will complete each sentence.

3. **Activity 2:** Ask the students to read the note Bob wrote to his friend Jack. Have them circle the incorrect plurals in the note. Ask them to write the correct plurals on the lines provided.

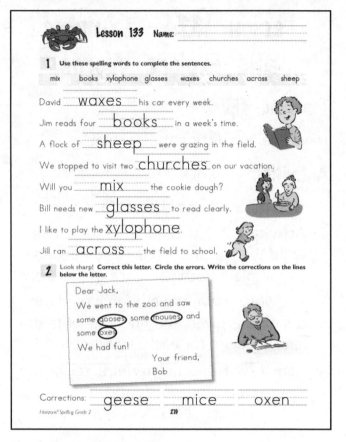

Extended Activities:

1. Give additional practice for students having difficulty with the plurals ending in **x**, **ch**, or **ss**.

2. Give additional practice for students having difficulty with irregular plurals.

3. Have the students continue the writing of sentences for each spelling word in their notebooks.

Lesson 134 - Apply Understanding of Words in Writing

Teaching Tips:

1. Have Spelling dictionaries available.
2. Have Bible story ready.

Activities:

1. Give the students Lesson 134.
2. **Writing Activity:** Read and discuss the parable of the lost sheep from Luke. Have the students retell the story in their own words and draw a picture to accompany it.

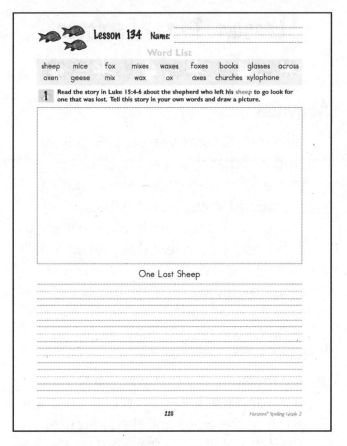

Extended Activities:

1. Share the students' pictures and rendering of the story.
2. Act out the story if time allows.
3. Have the students complete the writing of sentences for each spelling word in their notebooks.

Lesson 135 - Assess and Evaluate Progress

Activities:

1. Give the students Lesson 135. Tell the students that this is a "Check-up" page to see what they have learned during the week. [**Note:** Teachers/parents of home schoolers may decide what will be assessed. If a student does exceptionally well on the "What do you know?" pre-assessment, the teacher may choose not to test words already known by the student. Or the teacher may choose to test all words for the week.]

2. Tell the students that you will say a word and use it in a sentence. They will listen to the word and the sentence. Then they will write the word on the line next to the numbers. All working words are included in this review.

3. Say the word. Repeat it in the context of a sentence. Repeat the word.

4. The students write the word dictated.

5. The process is repeated until all words have been tested.

6. The teacher may correct in class by writing the words on the board and having the students compare or "self-correct" their work. Or the teacher may correct each student's work individually.

7. The teacher then writes any corrections for words misspelled in the space provided.

8. The students study the misspelled words, then practice them on the second side of the Lesson page.

9. Space is provided for retesting, for testing additional sight or "working words" added for the week, and for additional practice.

Check-up Time! Lesson 135 Name:

Spelling Test

1. _____ 11. _____
2. _____ 12. _____
3. _____ 13. _____
4. _____ 14. _____
5. _____ 15. _____
6. _____ 16. _____
7. _____ 17. _____
8. _____ 18. _____
9. _____ 19. _____
10. _____ 20. _____

Corrections

Horizons Spelling Grade 2   121

Extended Activity:

Review any words missed. Send words to review home for additional study. Praise all efforts.

Week 28

Lessons 136-140 - Assess Student's Knowledge

Goal: To recognize and spell the three different sounds of the ending **-ed**.

Review Rule: When a word ends in silent **e**, drop the **e** before adding a suffix that begins with a vowel. Examples: **hike/hiked**, **like/liked**.

What Do You Know?

Give the students the What do you know? page for Lessons 136-140. Tell them that this page will be used to see what they already know about the words for the week. Ask them to listen carefully to each word as you say it, repeat it in a sentence, and say it once again. Follow the procedures for this page as described in the *Introduction* at the beginning of this Teacher's Guide.

Show the children how to write their working words in the appropriate section at the back of their *Spelling Dictionary*.

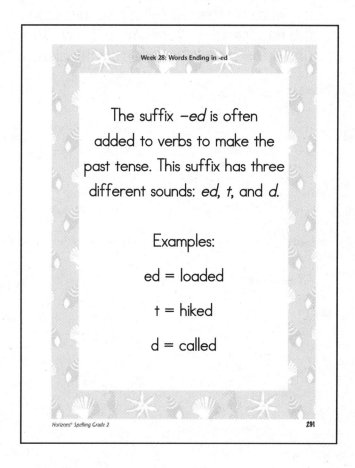

What do you know? Lessons 136-140 Name:

Words for the Week	Corrections	Practice
1. wanted		
2. tested		
3. waited		
4. melted		
5. loaded		
6. looked		
7. asked		
8. cooked		
9. mixed		
10. hiked		
11. played		
12. called		
13. used		
14. prayed		
15. cooled		
16. May		
17. June		

Horizons Spelling Grade 2   113

Week 28: Words Ending in -ed

The suffix *–ed* is often added to verbs to make the past tense. This suffix has three different sounds: *ed, t,* and *d.*

Examples:

ed = loaded

t = hiked

d = called

Horizons® Spelling Grade 2   291

Lesson 136 – Introduce Words

Activities:

1. Give the students Lesson 136.

2. Explain to the students that the suffix **-ed** is often added to verbs to make the past tense. The suffix **-ed** is also different in that it can take three different sounds: **ed**, **t**, and **d**. Most of the spelling words in this lesson end in **-ed**.

3. **Activity 1:** Have the students find and write the spelling words for each sound grouping of the **-ed** suffix.

4. **Activity 2:** Write the working words chosen for the week on the board. Ask the students to write all five of their working words for the week on the lines provided.

5. **Activity 3:** Students will write their working words in their Spelling dictionaries in the back section. Words are to be written under the correct letter of the alphabet.

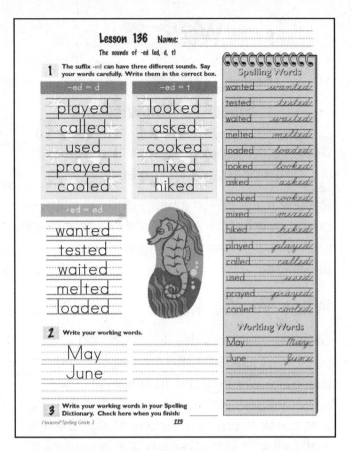

Extended Activities for the Week:

1. Send a list of the week's words home for further study. Emphasize the importance of using spelling words in sentences, in speech, in stories, etc., so that they are given a context and not simply memorized in isolation.

2. Assign reproducible *Week 28 Worksheet* either as homework or as an added classroom activity.

3. Have students write the definitions of the "choice" working words in their notebooks.

4. Have the students begin the writing of sentences for each spelling word in their notebooks.

5. Bring out or begin individual word family charts for each sound of the suffix **-ed**.

Lesson 137 - Examine and Explore Words

Activities:

1. Give the students Lesson 137.
2. **Activity 1:** Ask the students to find the correct spelling word needed to complete each sentence. The first letter is given for each.

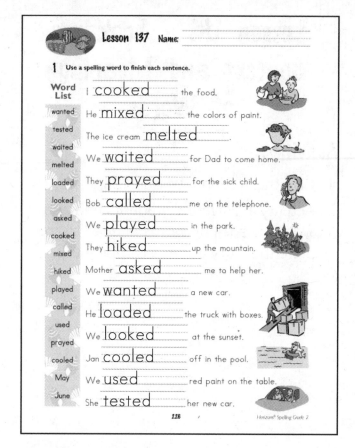

Extended Activity:

Have the students continue the writing of sentences for each spelling word in their notebooks.

Lesson 138 - Look at Context and Meaning of Words

Activities:

1. Give the students Lesson 138.
2. **Activity 1:** Have the students find and write the spelling words needed to complete the story about a camping trip.

Extended Activity:

Have the students continue the writing of sentences for each spelling word in their notebooks.

Lesson 139 - Apply Understanding of Words in Writing

Teaching Tip:

Have Spelling dictionaries available.

Activities:

1. Give the students Lesson 139.

2. **Writing Activity:** Talk about special days that happened with the last year. Ask the students to describe one such special day and draw a picture to illustrate it. Use as many spelling words as possible.

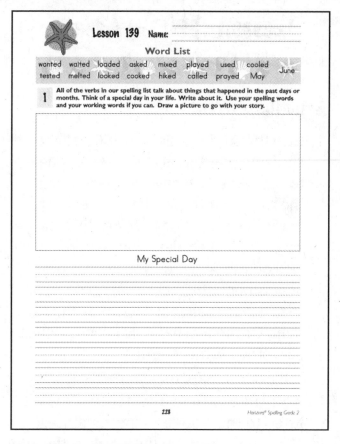

Extended Activities:

1. Share stories, pictures, and experiences.

2. Have the students complete the writing of sentences for each spelling word in their notebooks.

Lesson 140 - Assess and Evaluate Progress

Activities:

1. Give the students Lesson 140. Tell the students that this is a "Check-up" page to see what they have learned during the week. [**Note:** Teachers/parents of home schoolers may decide what will be assessed. If a student does exceptionally well on the "What do you know?" pre-assessment, the teacher may choose not to test words already known by the student. Or the teacher may choose to test all words for the week.]

2. Tell the students that you will say a word and use it in a sentence. They will listen to the word and the sentence. Then they will write the word on the line next to the numbers. All working words are included in this review.

3. Say the word. Repeat it in the context of a sentence. Repeat the word.

4. The students write the word dictated.

5. The process is repeated until all words have been tested.

6. The teacher may correct in class by writing the words on the board and having the students compare or "self-correct" their work. Or the teacher may correct each student's work individually.

7. The teacher then writes any corrections for words misspelled in the space provided.

8. The students study the misspelled words, then practice them on the second side of the Lesson page.

9. Space is provided for retesting, for testing additional sight or "working words" added for the week, and for additional practice.

Check-up Time! Lesson 140 Name:

Spelling Test

1.
2.
3.
4.
5.
6.
7.
8.
9.
10.
11.
12.
13.
14.
15.
16.
17.
18.
19.
20.

Corrections

Horizons® Spelling Grade 2   229

Extended Activity:

Review any words missed. Send words to review home for additional study. Praise all efforts.

Week 29

Lessons 141-145 - Assess Student's Knowledge

Goal: To recognize and spell number words.

What Do You Know?

Give the students the What do you know? page for Lessons 141-145. Tell them that this page will be used to see what they already know about the words for the week. Ask them to listen carefully to each word as you say it, repeat it in a sentence, and say it once again. Follow the procedures for this page as described in the *Introduction* at the beginning of this Teacher's Guide. [**Note:** This week's lesson has one extra working word.]

Show the children how to write their working words in the appropriate section at the back of their *Spelling Dictionary*.

What do you know!	Lessons 141-145	Name:
Words for the Week	**Corrections**	**Practice**

1. eleven
2. twelve
3. thirteen
4. fourteen
5. fifteen
6. sixteen
7. seventeen
8. eighteen
9. nineteen
10. twenty
11. thirty
12. forty
13. fifty
14. sixty
15. seventy
16. eighty
17. ninety
18. hundred

Horizons Spelling Grade 2   191

Lesson 141 - Introduce Words

Activities:

1. Give the students Lesson 141.

2. **Activity 1:** Have the students write the number spelling words for each numeral given.

3. **Activity 2:** Have the students write the number spelling words for each of the "teens" given.

4. **Activity 3:** Write the working words chosen for the week on the board. Ask the students to write all five of their working words for the week on the lines provided.

5. **Activity 4:** Students will write their working words in their Spelling dictionaries in the back section. Words are to be written under the correct letter of the alphabet.

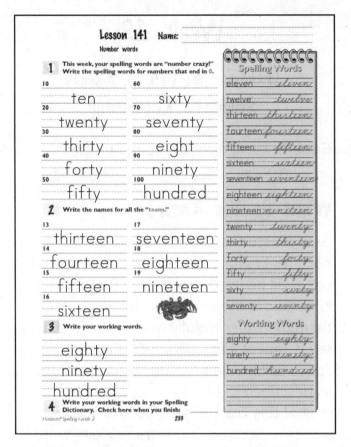

Extended Activities for the Week:

1. Send a list of the week's words home for further study. Emphasize the importance of using spelling words in sentences, in speech, in stories, etc., so that they are given a context and not simply memorized in isolation.

2. Assign reproducible *Week 29 Worksheet* either as homework or as an added classroom activity.

3. Have students write the definitions of the "choice" working words in their notebooks.

4. Have the students begin the writing of sentences for each spelling word in their notebooks.

5. Bring out or begin individual word family chart for number names.

Lesson 142 - Examine and Explore Words

Teaching Tip:

Have paper available to figure math problems.

Activities:

1. Give the students Lesson 142.

2. **Activity 1:** Act the students to find and circle the spelling words in the word search puzzle. Provide assistance for students with visual discrimination problems.

3. **Activity 2:** Have the students solve each math problem and use a spelling word to write the correct answer.

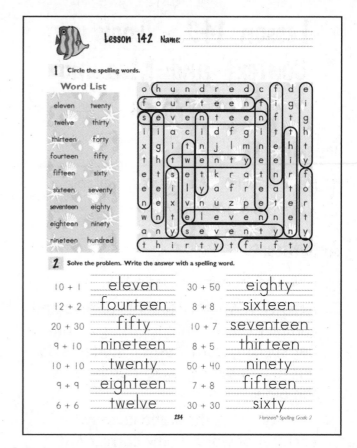

Extended Activities:

1. Give additional practice with spelling of number words as needed.

2. Have the students continue the writing of sentences for each spelling word in their notebooks.

Lesson 143 - Look at Context and Meaning of Words

Teaching Tips:

1. Have Spelling dictionaries available.
2. Have Bible or Bible verse ready.

Activities:

1. Give the students Lesson 143.
2. **Activity 1:** Ask the students to read and complete each sentence using a number spelling word. Assist if students do not remember the exact numbers from the Bible.
3. **Activity 2:** Ask the students to write each set of words in the correct ABC order.
4. **Activity 3:** Read the Bible verse with the students. Talk about older people they know. Have the students write a short paragraph about their grandparents.

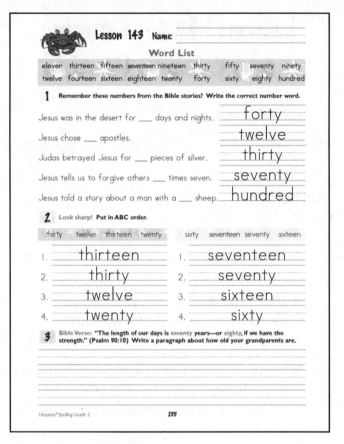

Extended Activities:

1. Discuss paragraphs.
2. Give additional help with ABC order of words if needed.
3. Have the students continue the writing of sentences for each spelling word in their notebooks.

Lesson 144 - Apply Understanding of Words in Writing

Teaching Tip:

Have Spelling dictionaries available.

Activities:

1. Give the students Lesson 144.

2. **Writing Activity:** Ask the students to think of an older person who is very special to them. The person may be an elderly grandparent, a neighbor, a friend, etc. Have the students draw a picture of the person and write a short story about their relationship with them.

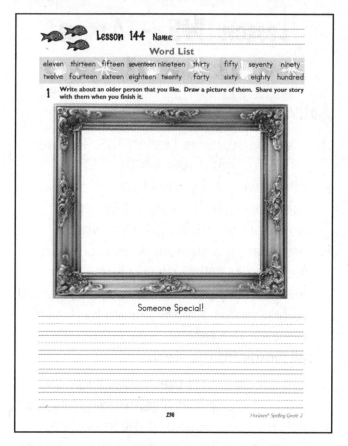

Extended Activities:

1. Share stories and picture with the class.

2. Write a note or send a copy of the story to the person.

3. Have the students complete the writing of sentences for each spelling word in their notebooks.

Lesson 145 - Assess and Evaluate Progress

Activities:

1. Give the students Lesson 145. Tell the students that this is a "Check-up" page to see what they have learned during the week. [**Note:** Teachers/parents of home schoolers may decide what will be assessed. If a student does exceptionally well on the "What do you know?" pre-assessment, the teacher may choose not to test words already known by the student. Or the teacher may choose to test all words for the week.]

2. Tell the students that you will say a word and use it in a sentence. They will listen to the word and the sentence. Then they will write the word on the line next to the numbers. All working words are included in this review.

3. Say the word. Repeat it in the context of a sentence. Repeat the word.

4. The students write the word dictated.

5. The process is repeated until all words have been tested.

6. The teacher may correct in class by writing the words on the board and having the students compare or "self-correct" their work. Or the teacher may correct each student's work individually.

7. The teacher then writes any corrections for words misspelled in the space provided.

8. The students study the misspelled words, then practice them on the second side of the Lesson page.

9. Space is provided for retesting, for testing additional sight or "working words" added for the week, and for additional practice.

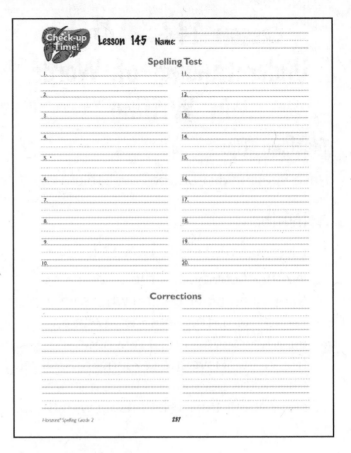

Extended Activity:

Review any words missed. Send words to review home for additional study. Praise all efforts.

Week 30

Lessons 146-150 - Assess Student's Knowledge

Goal: To recognize and spell words ending in **-le**.

Review Rules:

When a word ends in **le** preceded by a consonant, divide the word before that consonant. Examples: **bottle/bot-tle**, **scribble/scrib-ble**.

Guide words appear at the top of each dictionary page. They tell what the first and last words on the page are.

What Do You Know?

Give the students the What do you know? page for Lessons 146-150. Tell them that this page will be used to see what they already know about the words for the week. Ask them to listen carefully to each word as you say it, repeat it in a sentence, and say it once again. Follow the procedures for this page as described in the *Introduction* at the beginning of this Teacher's Guide.

Show the children how to write their working words in the appropriate section at the back of their *Spelling Dictionary*.

| What do you know? Lessons 146-150 | Name: |
| Words for the Week | Corrections | Practice |

1. bottle
2. juggle
3. nibble
4. bubble
5. giggle
6. puzzle
7. saddle
8. huddle
9. paddle
10. rattle
11. scribble
12. snuggle
13. riddle
14. kettle
15. puddle
16. morning
17. afternoon

Horizons Spelling Grade 2 199

Week 30: Words Ending in -le

When a word ends in *le* after a consonant, divide the word before that consonant.

Examples: bottle = bot–tle
scribble = scrib–ble

192 *Horizons® Spelling Grade 2*

Lesson 146 - Introduce Words

Activities:

1. Give the students Lesson 146.

2. Note that most of the spelling words in this unit end in **-le**. Ask the students to observe how many syllables are in each of the **-le** words. Note that most of the words have a double consonant in the middle of the word.

3. **Activity 1:** Have the students find and write the two spelling words that name different times during the day.

4. **Activity 2:** [**Note:** In activities 2 through 5, the students will be writing words in syllables. Each word space is divided into two sections.] Have the students find and write the three spelling words that have double **gg** in the middle.

5. **Activity 3:** Have the students find and write four of the spelling words that have double **dd** in the middle.

6. **Activity 4:** Have the students find and write the three spelling words that have double **tt** in the middle.

7. **Activity 5:** Have the students find and write the three spelling words that have double **bb** in the middle.

8. **Activity 6:** Write the working words chosen for the week on the board. Ask the students to write all five of their working words for the week on the lines provided.

9. **Activity 7:** Students will write their working words in their Spelling dictionaries in the back section. Words are to be written under the correct letter of the alphabet.

Extended Activities for the Week:

1. Send a list of the week's words home for further study. Emphasize the importance of using spelling words in sentences, in speech, in stories, etc., so that they are given a context and not simply memorized in isolation.

2. Assign reproducible *Week 30 Worksheet* either as homework or as an added classroom activity.

3. Have students write the definitions of the "choice" working words in their notebooks.

4. Have the students begin the writing of sentences for each spelling word in their notebooks.

5. Bring out or begin individual word family charts for **-le** words.

Lesson 147 – Examine and Explore Words

Activities:

1. Give the students Lesson 147.

2. **Activity 1:** Have the students draw lines to connect the puzzle pieces that go together to form a spelling word.

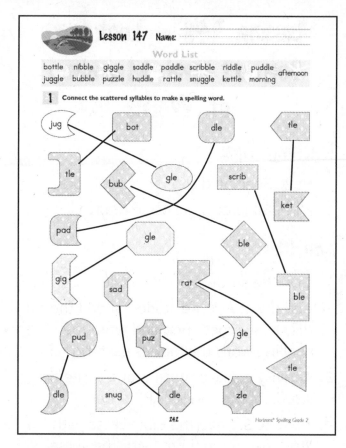

Extended Activity:

Have the students continue the writing of sentences for each spelling word in their notebooks.

Lesson 148 - Look at Context and Meaning of Words

Teaching Tips:

1. Have Spelling dictionaries available.
2. Have Bible or Bible verse ready.

Activities:

1. Give the students Lesson 148.
2. **Activity 1:** Ask the students read the riddles. Have them find and write the spelling word that solves each riddle.
3. **Activity 2:** Have the students write the words in the correct ABC order.
4. **Activity 3:** Read the Bible verse with the students. Have them learn the verse, copy it on their own paper, and share it with a friend.

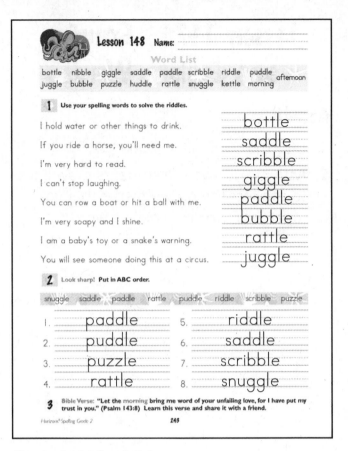

Extended Activities:

1. Give help with ABC order as needed.
2. Have the students continue the writing of sentences for each spelling word in their notebooks.

Lesson 149 - Apply Understanding of Words in Writing

Teaching Tips:

1. Have Spelling dictionaries available.
2. Have paper available so that students can write and illustrate a story when they have finished the questions.

Activities:

1. Give the students Lesson 149.
2. **Writing Activity:** Use the questions on this page as a pre-writing activity. Read and discuss the directions. Ask the students to use their imaginations to answer the questions given. Provide paper so that the students can write and illustrate their stories.

Lesson 149 Name:

Word List

bottle	nibble	giggle	saddle	paddle	scribble	riddle	puddle	
juggle	bubble	puzzle	huddle	rattle	snuggle	kettle	morning	afternoon

1 One day, two children found a bottle. Inside was a note that was scribbled on a piece of paper. Use your spelling words and your imagination when you answer the questions.

Where do you think the bottle came from?

Who do you think wrote the note?

What do you think the note said?

What do you think the children did with the bottle?

What would you do if you found a bottle with a note in it?

244   Horizons® Spelling Grade 2

Extended Activities:

1. Share stories and pictures with the class.
2. Make a bulletin board for the stories or a class book to put them in.
3. Have the students complete the writing of sentences for each spelling word in their notebooks.

Lesson 150 - Assess and Evaluate Progress

Activities:

1. Give the students Lesson 150. Tell the students that this is a "Check-up" page to see what they have learned during the week. [**Note:** Teachers/parents of home schoolers may decide what will be assessed. If a student does exceptionally well on the "What do you know?" pre-assessment, the teacher may choose not to test words already known by the student. Or the teacher may choose to test all words for the week.]

2. Tell the students that you will say a word and use it in a sentence. They will listen to the word and the sentence. Then they will write the word on the line next to the numbers. All working words are included in this review.

3. Say the word. Repeat it in the context of a sentence. Repeat the word.

4. The students write the word dictated.

5. The process is repeated until all words have been tested.

6. The teacher may correct in class by writing the words on the board and having the students compare or "self-correct" their work. Or the teacher may correct each student's work individually.

7. The teacher then writes any corrections for words misspelled in the space provided.

8. The students study the misspelled words, then practice them on the second side of the Lesson page.

9. Space is provided for retesting, for testing additional sight or "working words" added for the week, and for additional practice.

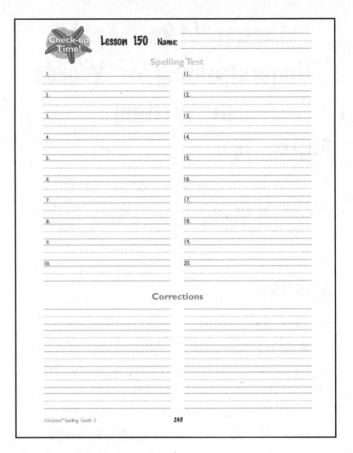

Extended Activity:

Review any words missed. Send words to review home for additional study. Praise all efforts.

Week 31

Lessons 151-155 - Assess Student's Knowledge

Goal: To recognize and spell words with the prefixes **un-** and **en-**.

Review Rules:

A prefix is a word part that is added at the beginning of a base word to change the base word's meaning or form a new word.

The prefix **un-** can mean "not" or "to change something."

The prefix **en-** means "cause to be" or "to make."

What Do You Know?

Give the students the What do you know? page for Lessons 151-155. Tell them that this page will be used to see what they already know about the words for the week. Ask them to listen carefully to each word as you say it, repeat it in a sentence, and say it once again. Follow the procedures for this page as described in the *Introduction* at the beginning of this Teacher's Guide.

Show the children how to write their working words in the appropriate section at the back of their *Spelling Dictionary*.

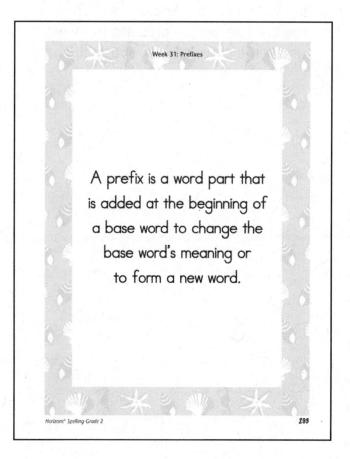

What do you know? Lessons 151-155   Name: _____

Words for the Week	Corrections	Practice
1. unpack		1.
2. unload		2.
3. undo		3.
4. uneasy		4.
5. unfair		5.
6. uneven		6.
7. unjust		7.
8. unlike		8.
9. unlock		9.
10. unkind		10.
11. entrust		11.
12. entire		12.
13. enlarge		13.
14. enclose		14.
15. enjoy		15.
16. tonight		16.
17. tomorrow		17.

Horizons Spelling Grade 2   147

Week 31: Prefixes

A prefix is a word part that is added at the beginning of a base word to change the base word's meaning or to form a new word.

Horizons® Spelling Grade 2   293

Lesson 151 - Introduce Words

Activities:

1. Give the students Lesson 151.

2. **Activity 1:** Explain to the students that the prefix **un-** has more than one meaning. In this activity, they will find and write spelling words in which the **un-** means "not."

3. **Activity 2:** In this activity, the students will find and write the spelling words in which the **un-** means "to change something."

4. **Activity 3:** Write the working words chosen for the week on the board. Ask the students to write all five of their working words for the week on the lines provided.

5. **Activity 4:** Students will write their working words in their Spelling dictionaries in the back section. Words are to be written under the correct letter of the alphabet.

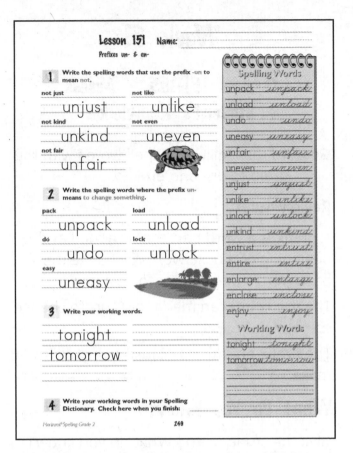

Extended Activities for the Week:

1. Send a list of the week's words home for further study. Emphasize the importance of using spelling words in sentences, in speech, in stories, etc., so that they are given a context and not simply memorized in isolation.

2. Assign reproducible *Week 31 Worksheet* either as homework or as an added classroom activity.

3. Have students write the definitions of the "choice" working words in their notebooks.

4. Have the students begin the writing of sentences for each spelling word in their notebooks.

5. Bring out or begin individual word family charts for words beginning with the prefixes **un-** and **en-**.

Lesson 152 - Examine and Explore Words

Teaching Tip:

Have Spelling dictionaries ready.

Activities:

1. Give the students Lesson 152.

2. **Activity 1:** Explain that the prefix **en-** can mean with or a condition. Have the students find and write the **en-** spelling words for each clue given.

3. **Activity 2:** Have the students read the sentence and decide which of the two words given best completes the sentence. When they have chosen, have them circle the correct word and write it in the sentence.

4. **Activity 3:** Have the students write the words in ABC order. Remind them that in this activity they will have to look to the third letter to determine the order.

5. **Activity 4:** Have the students find the words given in their Spelling dictionaries. Ask them to write the page number on which they found the word and the guide words.

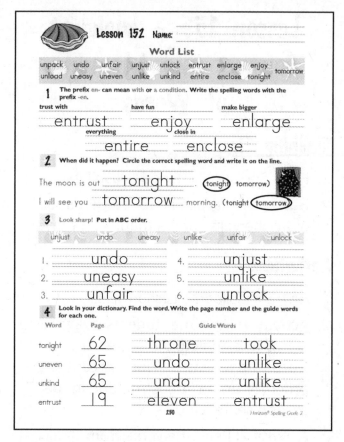

Extended Activities:

1. Have picture cards with words for different times of the day available in the learning center.

2. Give additional guide word practice as needed. Bring in larger dictionaries and show the students how the words are presented.

3. Have the students continue the writing of sentences for each spelling word in their notebooks.

Lesson 153 - Look at Context and Meaning of Words

Teaching Tips:

1. Have Spelling dictionaries available.
2. Have paper available for students to write the verse and a thank you prayer.

Activities:

1. Give the students Lesson 153.
2. **Activity 1:** Have the students use spelling words to complete the sentences. No words are repeated. [**Note:** Accept any order for **unfair/unjust/unkind** in the second sentence.]
3. **Activity 2:** Read the verse from Matthew. Discuss it with the students. Talk about some of the worries they may have and encourage them to entrust them to God's care. Say a prayer for all people who do not know God and do not entrust everything to him. Have the students write the verse on their own paper and write a prayer thanking God for his loving care.

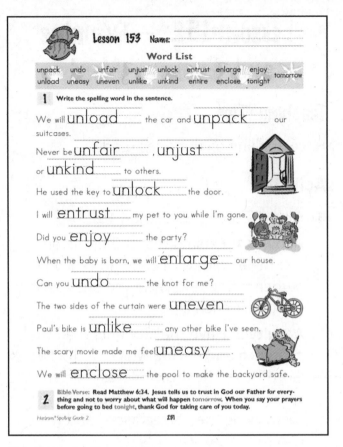

Extended Activities:

1. Do additional work with the spelling word meanings.
2. Have the students continue the writing of sentences for each spelling word in their notebooks.

Lesson 154 - Apply Understanding of Words in Writing

Teaching Tip:

Have Spelling dictionaries available.

Activities:

1. Give the students Lesson 154.
2. **Writing Activity:** Discuss things that you enjoy with the students. Ask them about things they enjoy doing. Have them write about some of the things they enjoy. Ask them to draw a picture about one of the things they enjoy.

Lesson 154 Name:

Word List

| unpack | undo | unfair | unjust | unlock | entrust | enlarge | enjoy | |
| unload | uneasy | uneven | unlike | unkind | entire | enclose | tonight | tomorrow |

1 Do you enjoy reading, or drawing, or painting? Do you enjoy singing or dancing? Do you enjoy playing in the rain, or snow, or sunshine best? Think about the things that you enjoy doing most. Write about them. Draw a picture of the thing you enjoy most.

Things I Enjoy

151

Horizons Spelling Grade 2

Extended Activities:

1. Share stories and pictures with the class.
2. Have the students complete the writing of sentences for each spelling word in their notebooks.

Lesson 155 - Assess and Evaluate Progress

Activities:

1. Give the students Lesson 155. Tell the students that this is a "Check-up" page to see what they have learned during the week. [**Note:** Teachers/parents of home schoolers may decide what will be assessed. If a student does exceptionally well on the "What do you know?" pre-assessment, the teacher may choose not to test words already known by the student. Or the teacher may choose to test all words for the week.]

2. Tell the students that you will say a word and use it in a sentence. They will listen to the word and the sentence. Then they will write the word on the line next to the numbers. All working words are included in this review.

3. Say the word. Repeat it in the context of a sentence. Repeat the word.

4. The students write the word dictated.

5. The process is repeated until all words have been tested.

6. The teacher may correct in class by writing the words on the board and having the students compare or "self-correct" their work. Or the teacher may correct each student's work individually.

7. The teacher then writes any corrections for words misspelled in the space provided.

8. The students study the misspelled words, then practice them on the second side of the Lesson page.

9. Space is provided for retesting, for testing additional sight or "working words" added for the week, and for additional practice.

Check-up Time! Lesson 155 Name: _____

Spelling Test

1.	11.
2.	12.
3.	13.
4.	14.
5.	15.
6.	16.
7.	17.
8.	18.
9.	19.
10.	20.

Corrections

Horizons® Spelling Grade 2   **155**

Extended Activity:

Review any words missed. Send words to review home for additional study. Praise all efforts.

Week 32

Lessons 156-160 - Assess Student's Knowledge

Goal: To review spelling words from Lessons 117-155.

Review Rules: Review all spelling rules.

What Do You Remember?

Give the students the What do you remember? page for Lessons 117-155. Tell them that this page will be used to see what they remember about the words they have studied so far this year. Select an additional four to six Working Words from the list of words added each week. Ask them to listen carefully to each word as you say it, repeat it in a sentence, and say it once again. Follow the procedures for this page as described in the Introduction at the beginning of this Teacher's Guide.

(NOTE: If you have kept records of words that each child continues to find difficult, you may want to adjust the words in this unit to fit the needs of the individual child. Replace review words already mastered with those still needing work.)

What do you remember?   Lessons 117-155   Name:

Write the words your teacher reads.

1. its
2. child's
3. hers
4. around
5. become
6. globe
7. please
8. clothes
9. foxes
10. geese
11. across
12. mice
13. prayed
14. used
15. asked
16. wanted
17. hundred
18. fifty
19. twenty
20. eleven
21. puzzle
22. morning
23. afternoon
24. bottle
25. tomorrow
26. tonight
27. unpack
28. enjoy

Horizons Spelling Grade 2   155

Lesson 156 - Introduce Words

Activities:

1. Give the students Lesson 156.

2. **Activity 1:** Have the students find and write the four plurals in this review unit.

3. **Activity 2:** Have the students find and write the three possessives in this review unit.

4. **Activity 3:** Have the students find and write the four number words in this review unit.

5. **Activity 4:** Have the students find and write the three review words that tell the time of day.

6. **Activity 5:** Have the students find and write the three I blend words in this review unit.

7. **Activity 6:** Have the students find and write the review word that means the next day.

8. **Activity 7:** Select, or have the students select, six of the CHOICE working words to be reviewed in this unit. The words may be chosen for the class, or on an individual basis according to the needs of the student. Ask the students to write the working words on the six lines provided.

Extended Activities for the Week:

1. Send a list of the week's words home for further study. Emphasize the importance of using spelling words in sentences, in speech, in stories, etc., so that they are given a context and not simply memorized in isolation.

2. Assign reproducible *Week 32 Worksheet* either as homework or as an added classroom activity.

3. Have students review the definitions of the "choice" working words in their notebooks.

4. Have the students review all the great work they have done through the year and all the sentences they have written for each spelling word in their notebooks.

5. Bring out all individual word family charts for the year.

Lesson 157 - Examine and Explore Words

Teaching Tip:

Have Spelling dictionaries available.

Activities:

1. Give the students Lesson 157.
2. **Activity 1:** Review the sounds of **-ed**. Have the students find and write the spelling word for each sound of **-ed**.
3. **Activity 2:** Have the students find and write the three three-syllable words. Ask them to draw a line between the syllables.
4. **Activity 3:** Have the students find and write fourteen two-syllable spelling words.
5. **Activity 4:** Have the students select three of the CHOICE review spelling words and write them in sentences.

Extended Activities:

1. This week is the final review for the entire year. Note each student's strengths and weaknesses and advise areas for review over the summer.
2. Read review word sentences aloud.

Lesson 158 - Look at Context and Meaning of Words

Teaching Tips:

1. Have Spelling dictionaries available.
2. Have pictures of activities that take place at different times of the day.

Activities:

1. Give the students Lesson 158.
2. **Activity 1:** Explain to the students that each sentence contains a review word that is misspelled. Have the students find the word and circle it. Ask them to write the correct spelling on the line provided. Help students with visual discrimination problems.
3. **Activity 2:** Discuss the questions. Have the students use spelling words to answer the questions with complete sentences.

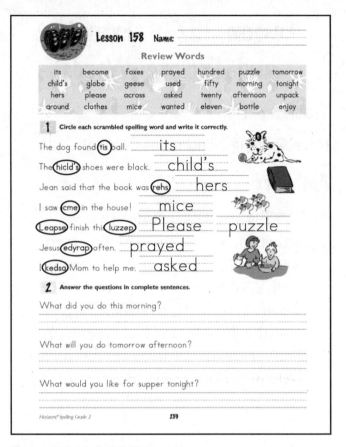

Extended Activities:

1. Share answers to the questions.
2. Give additional help and practice with scrambled words for those who need it.

Lesson 159 - Apply Understanding of Words in Writing

Teaching Tips:

1. Have Spelling dictionaries available.
2. Have a list of the Bible stories and verses covered throughout the year.

Activities:

1. Give the students Lesson 159.
2. **Writing Activity:** Review the Bible stories and verses covered throughout the year. Ask the students to select a favorite verse or story. Have them write about the story or copy the verse in their best writing. Have them decorate the border surrounding the writing.

Extended Activity:

Share stories and verses.

Lesson 160 - Assess and Evaluate Progress

Activities:

1. Give the students Lesson160. Tell the students that this is a "Check-up" page to see what they have learned during the week. [**Note:** Teachers/parents of home schoolers may decide what will be assessed. If a student does exceptionally well on the "What do you know?" pre-assessment, the teacher may choose not to test words already known by the student. Or the teacher may choose to test all words for the week.]

2. Tell the students that you will say a word and use it in a sentence. They will listen to the word and the sentence. Then they will write the word on the line next to the numbers. All working words are included in this review.

3. Say the word. Repeat it in the context of a sentence. Repeat the word.

4. The students write the word dictated.

5. The process is repeated until all words have been tested.

6. The teacher may correct in class by writing the words on the board and having the students compare or "self-correct" their work. Or the teacher may correct each student's work individually.

7. The teacher then writes any corrections for words misspelled in the space provided.

8. The students study the misspelled words, then practice them on the second side of the Lesson page.

9. Space is provided for retesting, for testing additional sight or "working words" added for the week, and for additional practice.

Check-up Time! | Lesson 160 | Name: _____

Spelling Test

1. _____ 18. _____
2. _____ 19. _____
3. _____ 20. _____
4. _____ 21. _____
5. _____ 22. _____
6. _____ 23. _____
7. _____ 24. _____
8. _____ 25. _____
9. _____ 26. _____
10. _____ 27. _____
11. _____ 28. _____
12. _____
13. _____
14. _____
15. _____
16. _____
17. _____

Horizons Spelling Grade 2   261

Extended Activities:

1. Review any words missed. Send words to review home for additional study. Praise all efforts.

2. Prepare a spelling evaluation for each student according to the strengths and weaknesses you have found. Go over with parents and offer suggestions for review over the summer break.

Reproducible Worksheets

Week 1 Worksheet

Lessons 1-5

Name:

Rule:

Many words are made of small parts called syllables. Each syllable has one vowel sound. Longer words are divided into parts called syllables.

1 Divide your spelling words into syllables.

batter _____ _____   water _____ _____

rubber _____ _____   mommy _____ _____

butter _____ _____   daddy _____ _____

ladder _____ _____   middle _____ _____

hammer _____ _____   cattle _____ _____

rabbit _____ _____   bitter _____ _____

pizza _____ _____   Monday _____ _____ ___ ___

letter _____ _____   September ___ ___ ___

lemon _____ _____

2 Write your "choice" working words and draw lines to divide them into syllables.

_____ _____ _____

_____ _____ _____

Week 2 Worksheet

Name: _____

Lessons 6-10

1 Cut the cards apart and arrange them in alphabetical order. Write a working word on the blank card.

math	sat	tan
map	path	winter
tip	win	sip
lip	summer	tug
tub	such	scrub
August	Sunday	

Week 3 Worksheet

Lessons 11-15

Word List

sock	pond	top	mop	pencil	leg	pet	hem	off
hot	nod	cob	met	men	belt	stem	second	

1 Use some of your spelling words to complete the crossword puzzles.

ACROSS:

1. A tame animal that lives with you.

2. This keeps your foot warm.

3. John broke his ____ when he fell.

4. Please ____ this skirt for me.

DOWN:

1. I need a sharper ____ .

2. That flower has a long ____ .

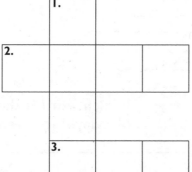

ACROSS:

2. John needs a new ____ for his shorts.

3. Please turn the radio ____ .

5. We have six fish in our ____ .

DOWN:

1. Matt is in the ____ grade.

4. As Mom sang softly, the baby began
   to ____ .

Week 4 Worksheet

Name: _____

Word List

| United | day | wait | bind | pine | smile | flew | new | y |
| States | clay | trail | sight | tile | huge | true | Saturda | July |

1 Write the long ū word that is the opposite.

old

_____

small

_____

false

_____

2 What two words spell the long ū sound with the letters "ew"?

_____   _____

3 Write the four words that begin with a capital letter.

_____   _____

_____   _____

4 Which word is the name of a summer month?

_____

5 Which word is the name of a dayof the week?

_____

6 Which two words name a country?

_____   _____

Week 5 Worksheet

Lessons 21-25

Name: _____

Word List

float	soap	foam	joke	wee	heat	seek	seen	believe
bone	rope	no	poke	we	wheat	meek	October	

1 Find two sets of long ō words that rhyme.

_____ _____ _____ _____

_____ _____ _____ _____

_____ _____ _____ _____

2 In your spelling list there are four ways to spell long ē: ea, _ee_, e, and _ie. Find and write the long ē words for each spelling.

ee	ea	e

ie

3 **EXTRA PRACTICE** – Can you think of any other words that you know for each of the long ē spellings? Write them here.

_____ _____ _____

_____ _____ _____

_____ _____ _____

_____ _____ _____

_____ _____ _____

_____ _____ _____

_____ _____ _____

Week 6 Worksheet

Lessons 26-30

Name: _____

Word List

somehow   headache   friendship   patchwork   foxhole

bedroom   forgot   meatloaf   someone

1 Use the words from the list to complete the crossword puzzle.

ACROSS:

2. The compound word formed by friend + ship.
4. The compound word formed by meat + loaf.
7. The compound word formed by some + one.
8. The compound word formed by some + how.

DOWN:

1. The room in which you sleep.
2. The compound word formed by fox + hole.
3. What you have when your head hurts.
5. A type of quilt for your bed.
6. "Oh no! I _____ to do my homework!"

Horizons Spelling Grade 2

Week 7 Worksheet

Lessons 31-35

Name: _____

Word List

fries	cross	brave	grade	cry	yak	yell	by	fifth
train	praise	dream	throne	trust	yam	baby	Wednesday	

1 Be a y detective. Find all the words in your spelling list in which the y is used as a consonant.

_____   _____   _____

_____   _____   _____

2 Look in the "Y" section of your Spelling Dictionary and write another word that uses y as a consonant.

_____

3 Can you think of any other words that you already know that use y as a consonant? Here are some hints:

A color   Opposite of "no"   The day before today

_____   _____   _____

_____   _____   _____

4 Look at the spelling words in which y is used as a vowel. Write them in the correct group, and ADD your own words to the list.

y = long ī   y = long ē

Week 8 Worksheet

Name: _____

Word List

middle	math	second	smile	believe	someone	by
Monday	winter	men	United States	seen	forgot	grade
letter	such	pencil	true	seek	bedroom	praise
water	Sunday	pet	new	we	friendship	trust

Friendship is very special. A friend is someone with whom you share happy times and sad times. A friend can make you smile. A friend can help you believe in yourself. Think about your best friend. Write a story about something you and your best friend have done. Use as many spelling words as you can. Draw a picture of you and your friend.

Week 9 Worksheet

Lessons 41-45

1 Cut the cards apart and arrange them in alphabetical order. Write a working word on the blank card.

shine	think	why
whose	chime	November
wish	thimble	whisper
chick	each	eighth
shout	both	while
chill	rich	

1 Cut out the leaves and paste them over the correct words on the "contraction tree" on the next page. When you have finished, you may color the picture.

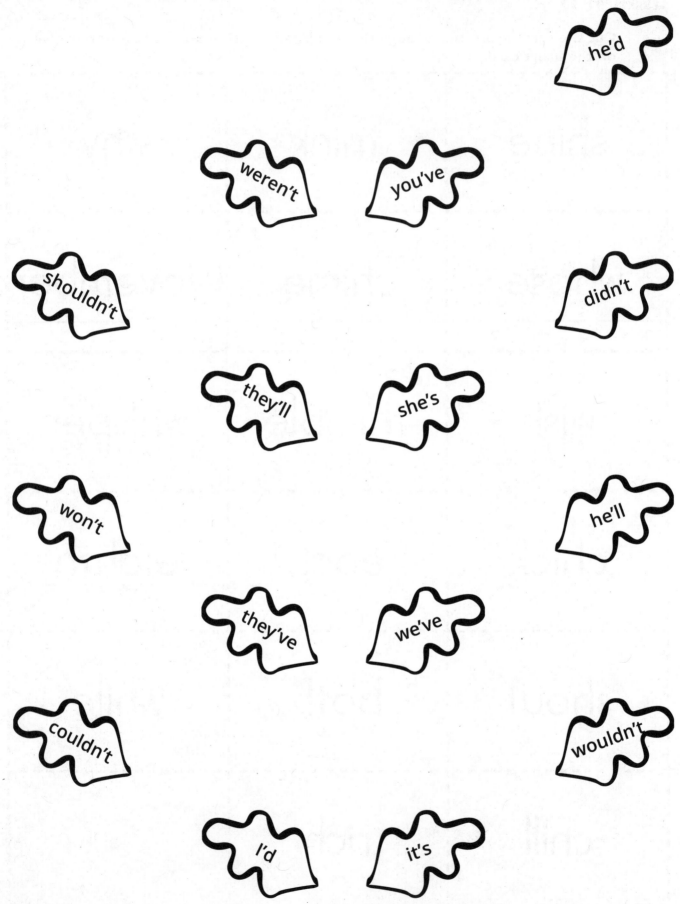

Contraction Tree

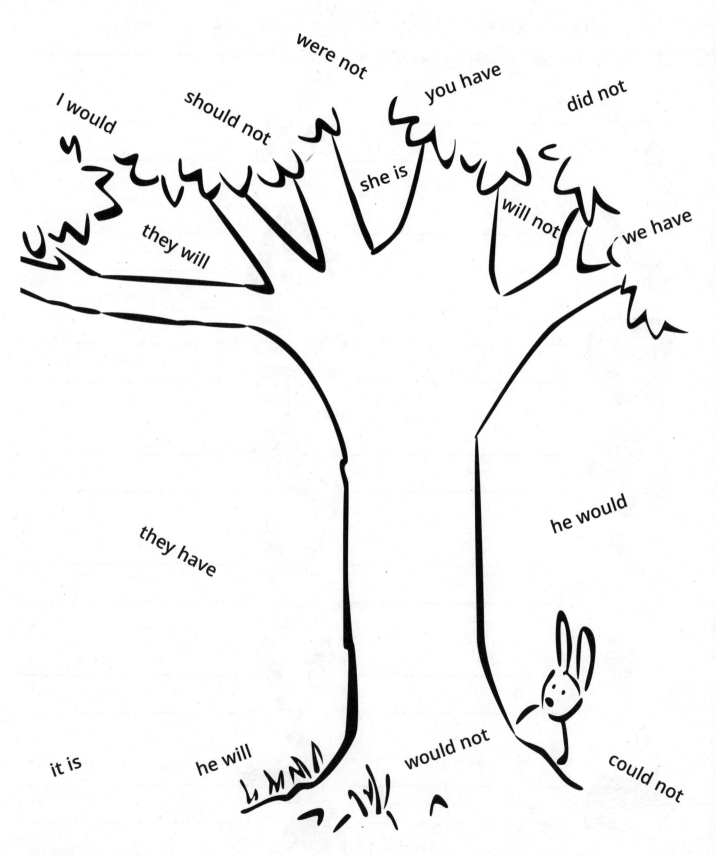

were not

should not

you have

did not

I would

she is

will not

they will

we have

they have

he would

it is

he will

would not

could not

Week 11 Worksheet

Lessons 51-55

Name: _____

Word List

life	knife	scarf	watches	houses	peaches	pets	puppies	tenth
lives	knives	scarves	wishes	torches	hands	kites	Thanksgiving

1 Write the correct spelling words for the pictures.

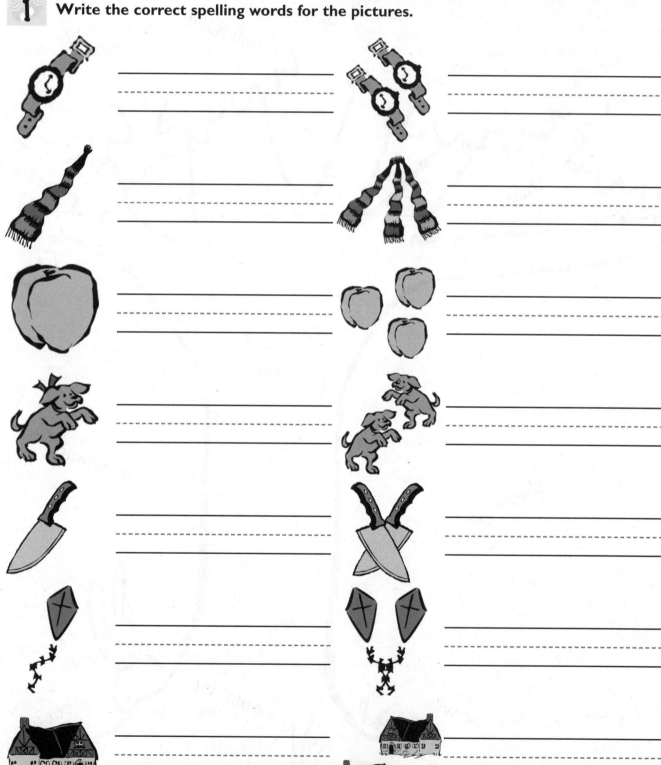

Week 12 Worksheet

Lessons 56-60

1 Use each set of words in a sentence.

tearful   helpless   thankful

---

wonderful   grateful   enjoyment

---

helpful   judgment   fearless

December   useful   handful

---

1   Cut the cards apart and arrange them in alphabetical order. Write a working word on the blank card.

rang	sang	hang
clang	thing	ring
sing	wing	song
strong	swing	string
rung	sung	lung
sixth	seventh	

Horizons Spelling Grade 2

Week 14 Worksheet

Lessons 66-70

Word List

cot	cut	center	circus	cage	ginger	gas	guess	begal
cuff	cape	circle	ice	giant	page	gum	before	

1   **WHAT AM I? Write the spelling words to match the definitions.**

I am the opposite of *ended*.

I am the opposite of *after*.

We rhyme with each other.

I am both a spice and a color.

I am completely round.

I am in the middle.

I am very, very tall.

I have lots of animals and clowns.

I am something you can chew.

I am used as fuel for a car.

I am a something you wear.

You can sleep on me.

I keep your drink cold.

I am found on a shirt sleeve.

Week 15 Worksheet

Lessons 71-75

Name: _____

Word List

hood	wool	stood	wood	spoon	goose	roof	noon	
shook	took	cook	boot	cool	pool	tool	beside	between

Read John 5:1-15 about a miracle by the pool. Write your own story about the miracle. Use as many spelling words as you can. Draw a picture of your favorite part of the story.

A Miracle by a Pool

Week 16 Worksheet

Lessons 76-80

Name: _____

Word List

think   whose   why   each   puppies

helpless   enjoyment   rung   before   page

ACROSS:

2. Baby dogs.
3. Part of a book.
5. A state of joy.
6. _____ coat is this?
9. What do you _____ about that?

DOWN:

1. Without help.
4. The opposite of after.
6. _____ did you do that?
7. Give _____ child a plate.
8. Ring, rang, _____ .

Week 17 Worksheet

Lessons 81-85

1 Find the vowel diphthong at the bottom of the page needed to complete each word. Cut out the correct spelling and paste it in the word.

cl____d   s____th   bl____

sl____   r____   c____nt

gr____   f____nd   cl____n

h____   w____   l____

t____n   pl____   m____th

ou	ou	ou	ou	ou	ow	ow

ow	ow	ow	ow	ow	ow	ow	ow

Week 18 Worksheet

Lessons 86-90

1 Find each spelling word and circle it. Write the words on the lines below.

Word List

nerve	verse	fur	dirt	stir	earth	world	word	
verb	curb	purse	sir	early	learn	work	below	inside

p	u	r	s	e	x	f	u	r
v	c	d	t	w	f	l	j	i
e	l	o	i	o	p	e	q	n
r	s	i	r	r	c	a	n	s
s	s	t	u	d	u	r	e	i
e	a	r	t	h	r	n	r	d
w	o	r	l	d	b	w	v	e
o	e	a	r	l	y	x	e	v
r	v	e	r	b	d	i	r	t
k	b	e	l	o	w	a	z	y

_____ _____ _____

_____ _____ _____

_____ _____ _____

_____ _____ _____

_____ _____ _____

_____ _____ _____

_____ _____ _____

_____ _____ _____

Name: _____

1 Cut the cards apart and arrange them in alphabetical order. Write a working word on the blank card.

stay	smart	spell
skate	clasp	splash
spray	script	squeak
stranger	stripe	swallow
must	snack	ask
outside	along	

Week 20 Worksheet

Lessons 96-100

1 Use the set of words given to write a short paragraph. Draw a picture for your paragraph.

deer   tale   dear   tail

_____

_____

_____

_____

_____

_____

_____

_____

_____

_____

_____

nose   hour   knows   our

_____

_____

_____

_____

_____

_____

_____

_____

_____

Week 21 Worksheet

Lessons 101-105

1 Arrange the following words in ABC order.

quilt   quiet   quest   quietly   quiz

1. _____   4. _____

2. _____   5. _____

3. _____

2 Think of a photograph that you like very much. Who is in that photograph?
Draw a picture of the photograph inside the frame. Write a few sentences about it.

My Favorite Photograph

_____
_____
_____
_____
_____
_____
_____
_____
_____
_____
_____

_____

Week 22 Worksheet

Lessons 106-110

Name: _____

1 **Using your Spelling Dictionary, find and write the guide words for the spelling words listed below.**

known

gnaw

science

supper

bees

dinner

needs

Christian

ache

photograph

Week 23 Worksheet

Lessons 111-115

1 **Circle the word in each row that is spelled correctly.**

1.	happyer	happier	hapier
2.	thiner	thinnier	thinner
3.	prettiest	pretyiest	prettyest
4.	bester	best	bestest
5.	littller	littlier	littler
6.	bigger	biggier	biger
7.	strongier	stronger	strongger
8.	betterer	bettier	better
9.	smallest	smalliest	smallerst
10.	happyiest	happiest	happyest

Horizons Spelling Grade 2

Week 24 Worksheet

Name: ----------------

Lessons 116-120

1 Cut the cards apart and arrange them in alphabetical order. Write a working word on the blank card.

Christian	scissors	here
smart	along	best
hear	alphabet	ask
better	world	slow
biggest	without	south
hour	count	

Week 25 Worksheet

Lessons 121-125

1   **Choose the correct word to complete the sentence. Circle it and write it on the line.**

1. The _____ hair was curly.
       boys   boy's

2. Jill went to help with the _____ story hour.
       children's   childrens

3. The baby _____ feathers were a bright yellow.
       ducks   duck's

4. This book is mine, but that book is _____ .
       theirs   their's

5. That little _____ mother has a nice voice.
       childs   child's

6. When the _____ sister got home, they ate supper.
       girl's   girls

7. The puppy lost _____ ball.
       it's   its

8. John's room is neater than _____ .
       hers   her's

9. The _____ edge was very sharp.
       rocks   rock's

10. Bob forgot to bring _____ lunch.
       his   he's

Week 26 Worksheet

Name: _____

Lessons 126-130

1 **Complete the crossword puzzle.**

ACROSS:

2. Did you see that big ___ of snow?

3. The caterpillar made a cocoon and ___ a butterfly.

5. We will have to ___ the pictures in the scrapbook.

DOWN:

1. Joe has a ___ for winning the race.

2. The candle ___ was bright.

3. What has ___ of Mark's bike?

4. What ___ will you wear to school?

5. A ___ is a small copy of the earth.

WORD LIST
- plan
- flake
- flame
- glue
- globe
- clothes
- became
- become

Week 27 Worksheet

Lessons 131-135

1 Circle the <u>plural</u> word in each row that is spelled correctly.

1.   sheep   sheeps

2.   glasss   glasses

3.   churches   churchs

4.   foxes   foxs

5.   waxs   waxes

6.   mixs   mixes

7.   axes   axs   axen

8.   oxes   oxen   oxs

9.   mouses   mice   mices

10.   gooses   geeses   geese

Horizons Spelling Grade 2

Week 28 Worksheet

Lessons 136-140

Word List

prayed	waited	wanted	tested
asked	looked	used	called

Jesus would often go away by himself to pray. Do you pray by yourself or with your family? What kinds of things do you pray for? Write about times you have prayed. Use some of the words in the box. Draw a picture to go with your story.

Week 29 Worksheet

Lessons 141-145

 Write the number word below the numeral given.

11	12	13
_____	_____	_____

14	15	16
_____	_____	_____

17	18	19
_____	_____	_____

20	30	40
_____	_____	_____

50	60	70
_____	_____	_____

80	90	100
_____	_____	_____

Horizons Spelling Grade 2

Week 30 Worksheet

Lessons 146-150

Name: _____

1 Use your Spelling Dictionary to find the guide words for each word listed. Write the page number and the two guide words.

	PAGE #	GUIDE WORD	GUIDE WORD
bottle	_____	_____	_____
giggle	_____	_____	_____
paddle	_____	_____	_____
riddle	_____	_____	_____
afternoon	_____	_____	_____
huddle	_____	_____	_____
saddle	_____	_____	_____
morning	_____	_____	_____
kettle	_____	_____	_____
juggle	_____	_____	_____

Name: _____

WORD LIST

unpack

undo

unjust

unlike

unkind

entrust

entire

enclose

enjoy

tonight

ACROSS:

1. The opposite of "pack."
2. Not like.
4. Take apart.
5. Everything.
6. The opposite of this morning.
7. Give someone the care of something.

DOWN:

1. Not just.
3. To take pleasure in.
4. Not kind.
5. Close in.

Horizons Spelling Grade 2

Week 32 Worksheet

Lessons 156-160

1 Draw a picture and write a sentence for each time of the day given.

Morning

_____
_____
_____

Afternoon

_____
_____
_____

Tonight

_____
_____
_____

Tomorrow

_____
_____
_____

Worksheet Answer Keys

Key for Week 1 Worksheet

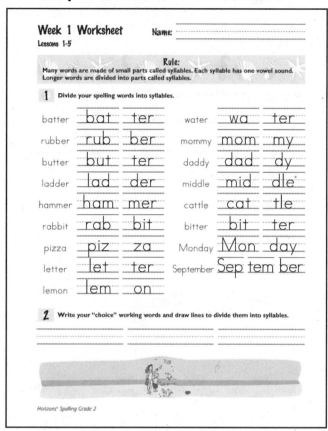

Week 1 Worksheet
Lessons 1-5

Name: _____

Rule:
Many words are made of small parts called syllables. Each syllable has one vowel sound. Longer words are divided into parts called syllables.

1 Divide your spelling words into syllables.

batter	bat	ter	water	wa	ter
rubber	rub	ber	mommy	mom	my
butter	but	ter	daddy	dad	dy
ladder	lad	der	middle	mid	dle
hammer	ham	mer	cattle	cat	tle
rabbit	rab	bit	bitter	bit	ter
pizza	piz	za	Monday	Mon	day
letter	let	ter	September	Sep tem ber
lemon	lem	on

2 Write your "choice" working words and draw lines to divide them into syllables.

_____ _____ _____
_____ _____ _____

Horizons® Spelling Grade 2

Key for Week 3 Worksheet

Week 3 Worksheet
Lessons 11-15

Name: _____

Word List

| sock | pond | top | mop | pencil | leg | pet | hem | off |
| hot | nod | cob | met | men | belt | stem | second | |

1 Use some of your spelling words to complete the crossword puzzles.

ACROSS:
1. A tame animal that lives with you.
2. This keeps your foot warm.
3. John broke his ____ when he fell.
4. Please ____ this skirt for me.
DOWN:
1. I need a sharper ____ .
2. That flower has a long ____ .

(crossword: p e t / p e n c i l / s o c k / s t e m / l e g / h e m)

ACROSS:
2. John needs a new ____ for his shorts.
3. Please turn the radio ____ .
5. We have six fish in our ____ .
DOWN:
1. Matt is in the ____ grade.
4. As Mom sang softly, the baby began to ____ .

(crossword: s / b e l t / s e c o n d / o f f / n / p o n d / d)

Horizons® Spelling Grade 2

Key for Week 4 Worksheet

Week 4 Worksheet
Lessons 16-20

Name: _____

Word List

| United | day | wait | bind | pine | smile | flew | new | July |
| States | clay | trail | sight | tile | huge | true | Saturday | |

1 Write the long ū word that is the opposite.

old   small
new   huge

false
true

2 What two words spell the long ū sound with the letters "ew"?

flew   new

3 Write the four words that begin with a capital letter.

United   Saturday
States   July

4 Which word is the name of a summer month?

July

5 Which word is the name of a day of the week?

Saturday

6 Which two words name a country?

United   States

Horizons® Spelling Grade 2

Key for Week 5 Worksheet

Week 5 Worksheet
Lessons 21-25

Name: _____

Word List

| float | soap | foam | joke | wee | heat | seek | seen | believe |
| bone | rope | no | poke | we | wheat | meek | October | |

1 Find two sets of long ō words that rhyme.

soap   rope   poke   joke

2 In your spelling list there are four ways to spell long ē: ea, _ee, e, and _ie. Find and write the long ē words for each spelling.

ee	ea	e
wee	heat	we
seek	wheat	
meek		**ie**
seen		believe

3 **EXTRA PRACTICE** – Can you think of any other words that you know for each of the long ē spellings? Write them here.

_____ _____
_____ _____
_____ _____
_____ _____
_____ _____
_____ _____

Horizons® Spelling Grade 2

Key for Week 6 Worksheet

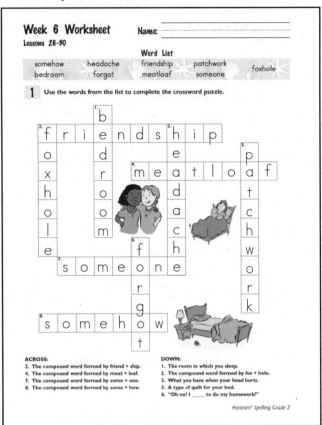

Key for Week 7 Worksheet

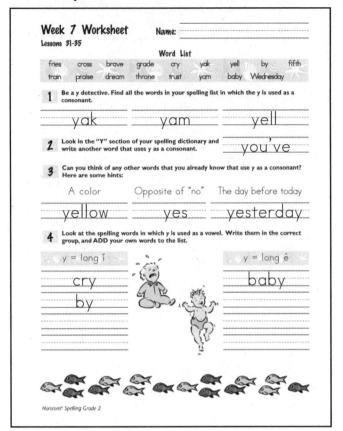

Key for Week 10 Worksheet

Key for Week 11 Worksheet

Key for Week 14 Worksheet

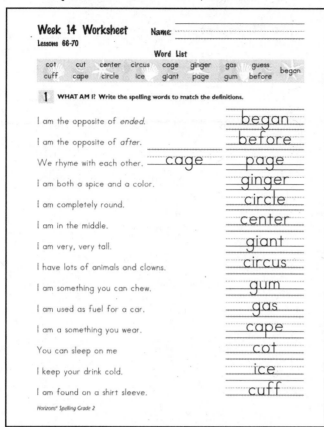

Week 14 Worksheet
Lessons 66-70

Name: _____

Word List

| cot | cut | center | circus | cage | ginger | gas | guess | began |
| cuff | cape | circle | ice | giant | page | gum | before | |

1 WHAT AM I? Write the spelling words to match the definitions.

I am the opposite of *ended*.   began
I am the opposite of *after*.   before
We rhyme with each other. cage   page
I am both a spice and a color.   ginger
I am completely round.   circle
I am in the middle.   center
I am very, very tall.   giant
I have lots of animals and clowns.   circus
I am something you can chew.   gum
I am used as fuel for a car.   gas
I am a something you wear.   cape
You can sleep on me.   cot
I keep your drink cold.   ice
I am found on a shirt sleeve.   cuff

Horizons® Spelling Grade 2

Key for Week 16 Worksheet

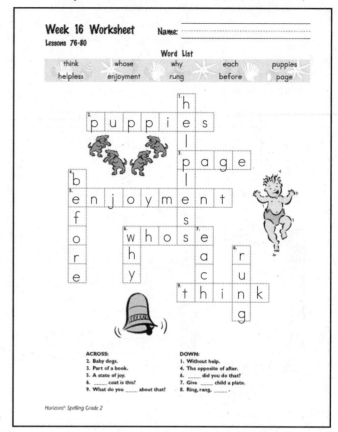

Week 16 Worksheet
Lessons 76-80

Name: _____

Word List

| think | whose | why | each | puppies |
| helpless | enjoyment | rung | before | page |

ACROSS:
2. Baby dogs.
3. Part of a book.
5. A state of joy.
6. _____ coat is this?
9. What do you _____ about that?

DOWN:
1. Without help.
4. The opposite of after.
6. _____ did you do that?
7. Give _____ child a plate.
8. Ring, rang, _____.

Horizons® Spelling Grade 2

Key for Week 17 Worksheet

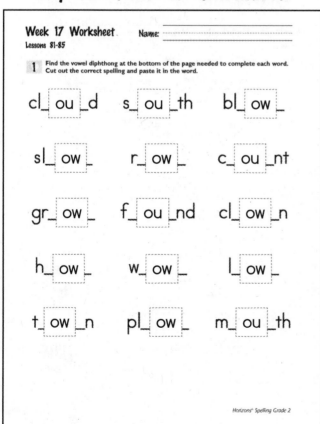

Week 17 Worksheet
Lessons 81-85

Name: _____

1 Find the vowel diphthong at the bottom of the page needed to complete each word. Cut out the correct spelling and paste it in the word.

cl_ ou _d   s_ ou _th   bl_ ow _

sl_ ow _   r_ ow _   c_ ou _nt

gr_ ow _   f_ ou _nd   cl_ ow _n

h_ ow _   w_ ow _   l_ ow _

t_ ow _n   pl_ ow _   m_ ou _th

Horizons® Spelling Grade 2

Key for Week 18 Worksheet

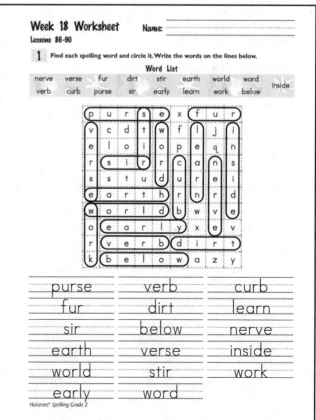

Week 18 Worksheet
Lessons 86-90

Name: _____

1 Find each spelling word and circle it. Write the words on the lines below.

Word List

| nerve | verse | fur | dirt | stir | earth | world | word | inside |
| verb | curb | purse | sir | early | learn | work | below | |

purse	verb	curb
fur	dirt	learn
sir	below	nerve
earth	verse	inside
world	stir	work
early	word	

Horizons® Spelling Grade 2

Key for Week 21 Worksheet

Week 21 Worksheet   Name: _____
Lessons 101-105

1 Arrange the following words in ABC order.

quilt   quiet   quest   quietly   quiz

1. quest   4. quilt
2. quiet   5. quiz
3. quietly

2 Think of a photograph that you like very much. Who is in that photograph? Draw a picture of the photograph inside the frame. Write a few sentences about it.

My Favorite Photograph

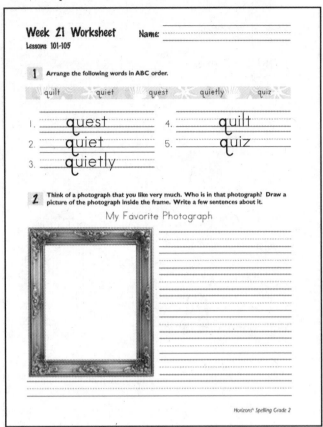

Key for Week 22 Worksheet

Week 22 Worksheet   Name: _____
Lessons 106-110

1 Using your spelling dictionary, find and write the guide words for the spelling words listed below.

known	knives	knows
gnaw	glasses	goose
science	scene	second
supper	strong	supper
bees	bees	better
dinner	daddy	dirt
needs	needs	nod
Christian	chill	circus
ache	ache	ant
photograph	pet	pizza

Key for Week 23 Worksheet

Week 23 Worksheet   Name: _____
Lessons 111-115

1 Circle the word in each row that is spelled correctly.

1. happyer — (happier) — hapier
2. thiner — thinnier — (thinner)
3. (prettiest) — pretyiest — prettyest
4. bester — (best) — bestest
5. littller — littlier — (littler)
6. (bigger) — biggier — biger
7. strongier — (stronger) — strongger
8. betterer — bettier — (better)
9. (smallest) — smalliest — smallerst
10. happyiest — (happiest) — happyest

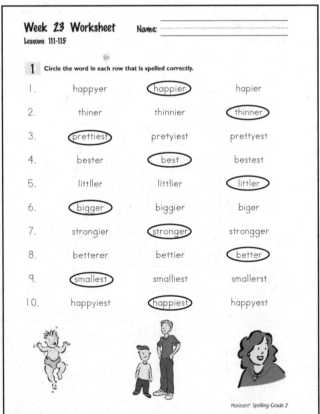

Key for Week 25 Worksheet

Week 25 Worksheet   Name: _____
Lessons 121-125

1 Choose the correct word to complete the sentence. Circle it and write it on the line.

1. The **boy's** hair was curly.
   boys / boy's

2. Jill went to help with the **children's** story hour.
   children's / childrens

3. The baby **duck's** feathers were a bright yellow.
   ducks / duck's

4. This book is mine, but that book is **theirs**
   theirs / their's

5. That little **child's** mother has a nice voice.
   childs / child's

6. When the **girl's** sister got home, they ate supper.
   girl's / girls

7. The puppy lost **its** ball.
   it's / its

8. John's room is neater than **hers**
   hers / her's

9. The **rock's** edge was very sharp.
   rocks / rock's

10. Bob forgot to bring **his** lunch.
    his / he's

Key for Week 26 Worksheet

Week 26 Worksheet
Lessons 126-130

Name: _____

1 Complete the crossword puzzle.

ACROSS:
2. Did you see that big ___ of snow?
3. The caterpillar made a cocoon and ___ a butterfly.
5. We will have to ___ the pictures in the scrapbook.

DOWN:
1. Joe has a ___ for winning the race.
2. The candle ___ was bright.
3. What has ___ of Mark's bike?
4. What ___ will you wear to school?
5. A ___ is a small copy of the earth.

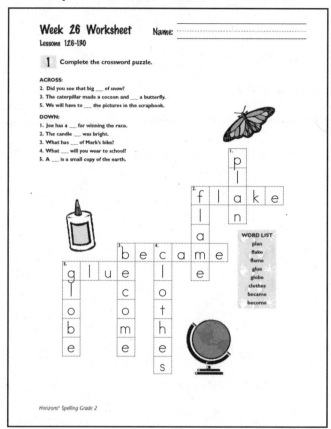

WORD LIST
plan
flake
flame
glue
globe
clothes
became
become

Crossword answers:
- plan
- flake
- flame
- became
- glue
- globe
- clothes
- become

Horizons® Spelling Grade 2

Key for Week 27 Worksheet

Week 27 Worksheet
Lessons 131-135

Name: _____

1 Circle the **plural** word in each row that is spelled correctly.

1. (sheep)   sheeps
2. glasss   (glasses)
3. (churches)   churchs
4. (foxes)   foxs
5. waxs   (waxes)
6. mixs   (mixes)
7. (axes)   axs   axen
8. oxes   (oxen)   oxs
9. mouses   (mice)   mices
10. gooses   geeses   (geese)

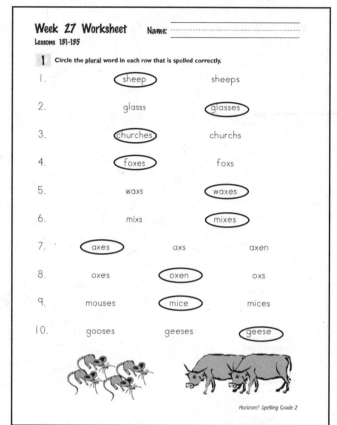

Horizons® Spelling Grade 2

Key for Week 29 Worksheet

Week 29 Worksheet
Lessons 141-145

Name: _____

1 Write the number word below the numeral given.

11	12	13
eleven	twelve	thirteen
14	15	16
fourteen	fifteen	sixteen
17	18	19
seventeen	eighteen	nineteen
20	30	40
twenty	thirty	forty
50	60	70
fifty	sixty	seventy
80	90	100
eighty	ninety	hundred

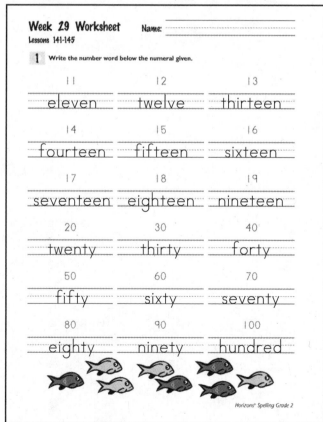

Horizons® Spelling Grade 2

Key for Week 30 Worksheet

Week 30 Worksheet
Lessons 146-150

Name: _____

1 Use your spelling dictionary to find the guide words for each word listed. Write the page number and the two guide words.

	PAGE #	GUIDE WORD	GUIDE WORD
bottle	8	blow	boy's
giggle	23	gas	glad
paddle	41	paddle	pencil
riddle	48	riddle	roughly
afternoon	3	ache	ant
huddle	28	hood	hundred
saddle	50	sack	scarves
morning	37	mop	must
kettle	31	kettle	knight
juggle	30	January	June

Horizons® Spelling Grade 2

Key for Week 31 Worksheet

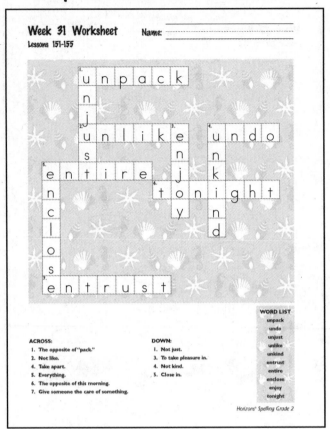

Week 31 Worksheet
Lessons 151-155

Name: _____

The crossword puzzle solution:

1. unpack
2. unlike
4. undo
5. entire
6. tonight
7. entrust

Down words: unjust, enjoy, unkind, enclose

ACROSS:
1. The opposite of "pack."
2. Not like.
4. Take apart.
5. Everything.
6. The opposite of this morning.
7. Give someone the care of something.

DOWN:
1. Not just.
3. To take pleasure in.
4. Not kind.
5. Close in.

WORD LIST
unpack
undo
unjust
unlike
unkind
entrust
entire
enclose
enjoy
tonight

Horizons® Spelling Grade 2

Reproducible Phonics Rules Flashcards

■──────────────────────────────────────■

Vowels:

a, e, i, o, u, and

sometimes *y* and *w.*

Consonants:

all the other letters

of the alphabet, and

usually *y.*

Many words are made of small parts called syllables. Each syllable has one vowel sound.

A one-syllable word is never divided.

When two or more consonants come between two or more vowels in a word, usually divide the word *after* the consonant if the first vowel is *short*.

When a single consonant comes between two long vowels in a word, usually divide the word *before* the consonant if the first vowel is *long*.

When a word or syllable has only one vowel, and it comes between two consonants or at the beginning of a word or syllable, the vowel is usually *short*.

Examples: ăt, măn, pĕt, pĭn, fŭn.

The symbol for the short vowel sound is called a *breve* (˘).

Names of people, months, days of the week, and special places begin with a capital letter.

Examples: John, Monday, United States

When a word or syllable has two vowels, the first vowel is usually long, and the second vowel is usually *silent*.

Examples: nāmé, pāín, pāý, tīmé, pīé, blūé, bōát, pēék

The symbol for the long vowel sound is called a *macron* (⁻).

When a word or syllable has just one vowel, and the vowel comes at the end of the word or syllable, the vowel sound is usually *long*.

Examples: be, go, Tony

A compound word is a word made from two or more words joined together to make one word.

Examples: backyard, runway, mailbox

A compound word is divided between the words that make up the compound word.

In an *r* blend, two or more consonants come together in a word. Their sounds blend together, but each sound is heard.

Examples: green, frog, tree

Sometimes *y* can stand for the vowel sound of long *ē* or long *ī*. When *y* is the only vowel at the end of a one–syllable word, *y* usually has the long *ī* sound.
Examples: my, by

When *y* is the only vowel at the end of a word of more than one syllable, *y* usually has the long *ē* sound
Examples: baby, lazy

A consonant digraph is two or more consonants that stay together to make their special sound.

Examples: shoe, three, chair, watch, when

The consonant digraph *ch* makes the sound as in the beginning of chair.

Examples: chair, choose, kitchen, watch, stitch.

The *ch* can also make the *k* sound.

Example: chorus

In consonant digraph *wh*, the *wh* makes the *w* sound.

Examples: what, when

A contraction is a short way to write two words as one. When the two words are put together, one or more letters are left out. A sign called an apostrophe (') is used to show where the letters were left out.

Examples:

they will = they'll

I have = I've

could not = couldn't

Plural means "more than one." Many plurals are formed by adding *-s* to the word.

Examples: trucks, cars, plates, things

If a word ends in *ss, x, ch,* or *sh*, add the suffix *-es* to make the word plural.

If a word ends in *f* or *fe*, usually change the *f* or *fe* to v before adding the suffix −*es*.

Examples:

knife − fe + v + es = knives

scarf − f + v + es = scarves

When a word ends in *y* after a consonant, usually change the *y* to an *i* before adding *–es.*

Examples:

baby – y + i + es = babies

puppy – y + i + es = puppies

Base words are words that
do not have a
prefix (beginning)
or suffix (ending)
added to them.

A suffix is an ending
that is added to a word
to make a new word.

Usually when the suffixes
-ful, *-less*, or *-ment*
are added, the spelling of the
base word does *not* change.

Examples: painful, hopeless,
enjoyment

When *c* is followed by *e, i,*
or *y,* it makes the *soft* sound,
as in the word "city."

When *c* is followed by *a, u, o,*
or a consonant, it makes
the *hard* sound, as in
the word "cat."

When *g* is followed by *e*, *i*, or *y*, it makes the *soft* sound, as in the word "giraffe."

When *g* is followed by *a*, *u*, *o*, or a consonant, it makes the *hard* sound, as in the word "gum."

Vowel digraphs are two vowels put together in a word that make a long or short sound, or have a special sound all their own.

The vowel digraph *oo* can stand for the vowel sound heard in book or in pool.

A vowel diphthong is two vowels that blend together to make one sound.

The diphthongs *ow* and *ou* stand for the sounds heard in out, brown, and snow.

The diphthong *ow* can make two sounds: *ow* as in cow, or *ow* as in snow.

An *r* after a vowel makes the
vowel sound different from
a short or long sound.

Examples: her, clerk, letter,
first, dirt, nurse, fur, burn,
work, early.

In an *s* blend, two or more consonants come together in a word. Their sounds blend together, but each sound is heard.

Examples: spell, snail

Homophones are words that sound alike but have different spellings and different meanings.

Examples: knows–nose, read–reed, bear–bare

The letters *qu* stand
for the *kw* sound.

Examples: quiet, quilt

The letters *ph* and *gh* can stand for the *f* sound.

Examples: laugh, rough, phone, elephant

The consonant digraphs *gn* and *kn* stand for the *n* sound. The *g* and *k* are silent.

Examples sign, gnaw, knife

The consonant digraph *sc* sometimes stands for the *s* sound. The *c* is silent.

Examples: science, scent

Guide words appear at the top of each dictionary page. They tell what the first and last words on the page are.

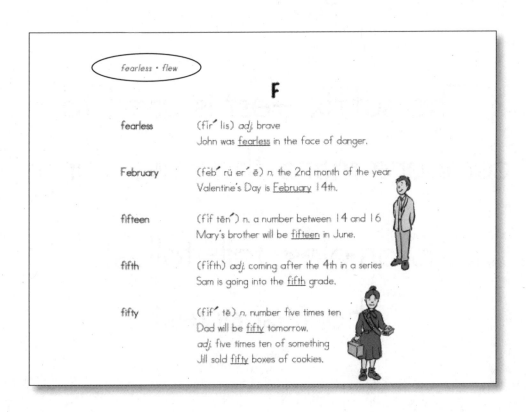

The suffix *-er* can be used to compare two things.

Examples: near-nearer, long-longer, short-shorter

The suffix *-est* is used to compare more than two things.

Examples: tall-tallest, short-shortest

When a word ends in *y* after a consonant, change the *y* to *i* before adding *er* or *est* to the end.

Examples:

pretty – y + i + er = prettier

happy – y + i + est = happiest

If a word with a short vowel sound ends in a single consonant, usually double the consonant before adding a suffix that begins with a vowel.

Examples:

big + g + er = bigger

fat + t + est = fattest

If a word ends in silent *e*, drop the *e* before adding a suffix that begins with a vowel.

Examples:

write – e + er = writer

little – e + est = littlest

hike – e + ed = hiked

To make a singular noun show possession, add an apostrophe and an *s* (*'s*) at the end of the word.

Examples: boy's, child's

When a noun ends in *s*, add an apostrophe at the end of the word.
Example: Jesus'

In an *l* blend, two or more consonants come together in a word. Their sounds blend together, but each sound is heard.

Examples: black, plant, sled

If a word ends in *x, ch*, or *ss*, add the suffix –*es* to make the word plural.

Examples:

fox + es = foxes

church + es = churches

class + es = classes

The suffix *-ed* is often added to verbs to make the past tense. This suffix has three different sounds: *ed, t,* and *d.*

Examples:

ed = loaded

t = hiked

d = called

When a word ends in *le* after a consonant, divide the word before that consonant.

Examples: bottle = bot–tle
scribble = scrib–ble

A prefix is a word part that is added at the beginning of a base word to change the base word's meaning or to form a new word.

The prefix *un–* can mean *not*.

Examples: uneasy, unkind

The prefix *un–* can also mean *to change something*.

Examples: unlock, unload

The prefix *en–* means *cause to be* or *to make.*

Examples: enjoy, enlarge

Cumulative Word List
Spelling 1 & 2

A

a	afternoon	always	April	ate
about	airplane	am	are	August
ache	airport	an	arm	aunt
across	all	and	around	ax
add	along	ant	ask	axes
after	alphabet	anyone	asked	

B

baby	been	beyond	bluff	brave
back	bees	big	boat	bread
ball	before	bigger	boil	break
bare	began	biggest	bone	breakfast
baseball	begging	bind	book	brother
batter	behind	bird	books	brown
be	believe	birthday	boot	bubble
beaches	bell	bitter	both	burn
bear	below	black	bottle	but
became	belt	blame	bowl	butter
because	beside	blend	box	butterfly
become	best	bless	boxes	by
bed	better	blow	boy	
bedroom	between	blue	boy's	

C

cage	chick	circus	cloud	could
called	child	circle	clown	couldn't
calling	children	city	cob	count
came	child's	clang	cold	cross
can	children's	clasp	come	cry
can't	chill	class	cook	cuff
cape	chime	classes	cooked	cupful
car	chin	clay	cool	curb
cat	Christ	click	cooled	cut
cattle	Christian	climb	cot	cute
cent	Christmas	clock	cough	
center	church	clothes		

D

daddy	did	do	door	drop
day	didn't	dock	down	duck
dear	dinner	does	dream	
December	dirt	dolls	dresses	
deer	dishes	don't		

E

each	echo	eighty	enjoyment	every
early	eggs	elephant	enlarge	eye
earth	eight	eleven	entire	
Easter	eighteen	enclose	entrust	
eat	eighth	enjoy		

farm	find	fly	forty	Friday
faster	first	foam	found	friend
fastest	five	food	four	friendship
fearless	fix	foot	fourteen	fries
February	flake	football	fourth	frog
feet	flame	for	fox	from
fifteen	flew	forget	foxes	fur
fifth	float	forgetful	foxhole	
fifty	flower	forgot	free	

gas	girl	glue	God	grateful
gate	giggle	gnash	good	green
geese	ginger	gnat	goodness	grow
gentle	girl's	gnaw	goose	guess
get	glad	gnome	gopher	gum
giant	glass	go	grade	
gift	globe	goat		

H

hammer	haven't	her	home	house
handful	he	here	hood	houses
hands	head	hers	hop	how
hang	headache	hide	hope	huddle
happier	hear	high	hopeless	huge
happiest	he'd	higher	hoping	hugged
happiness	he'll	highest	hopped	hugging
happy	helpful	hiked	hopping	hundred
hard	helpless	him	hot	
have	hem	his	hour	

I

I	I'll	its	in	itch
ice	I'm	it's	it	
I'd	inside	I've		

J

January	joke	judgment	July	just
Jesus	joy	juggle	June	
join	joyful			

K

kettle	kindness	kneel	knight	know
kind	kites	knees	knives	knows
kinder	kneads	knew	knock	known
kindest	knee	knife	knot	

Horizons Spelling Grade 2

L

lad	leg	like	lock	love
ladder	lemon	lip	long	low
lamb	less	little	longer	luck
lass	letter	littler	longest	lunch
latch	lick	littlest	look	lunches
laugh	life	lives	looked	lung
learn	light	loaded	looking	

M

made	May	met	mom	mouth
mail	me	mice	mommy	Mr.
mailman	meal	middle	Monday	Mrs.
make	meat	mile	moon	much
many	meatloaf	mine	moonlight	must
map	meek	miss	mop	my
March	meet	mix	morning	
match	melted	mixed	most	
math	men	mixes	mother	

N

needs	nice	ninth	nose	nowhere
nerve	night	no	not	nurse
never	nine	nod	November	
new	nineteen	noise	now	
nibble	ninety	noon		

O

October	on	other	over
off	one	out	ox
old	or	outside	oxen

P

pack	peaches	photo	play	prayed
paddle	peak	photograph	played	present
page	peek	pick	playful	prettiest
park	pen	pie	please	pretty
part	pencil	pine	plow	puddle
patch	people	pitch	poke	puppies
patchwork	pet	pizza	pond	purple
path	pets	plan	pool	purse
Paul	phone	plant	praise	puzzle
peace	phonics	plate	pray	

Q

quack	quest	quiet	quilt	quiz
queen	quick	quietly	quit	

R

rabbit	reaches	right	roof	rubber
rain	read	ring	rope	run
rainbow	reed	road	rough	rung
rang	rich	rock	roughly	
rattle	riddle	rode	row	

sack	September	sing	snow	stone
saddle	serve	sip	snuggle	stood
said	seven	sir	so	stop
sail	seventeen	sixteen	soap	store
sang	seventh	sixth	sock	story
sat	seventy	sixty	softer	stove
Saturday	shall	skate	softest	stranger
saw	she	skip	some	straw
say	she's	skirt	somehow	street
scarf	sheep	sky	someone	string
scarves	shell	sleep	something	stripe
scene	shine	slip	song	strong
scent	ship	slow	south	stronger
school	shirt	small	speak	strongest
science	shoe	smaller	spell	such
scissors	shoeless	smallest	spelling	summer
scribble	shook	smart	splash	Sunday
script	short	smell	spoon	sung
scrub	should	smile	spray	supper
sea	shouldn't	smiling	squeak	swallow
second	shout	smoke	stay	swing
see	sick	snack	stem	
seek	sight	snail	stick	
seen	sign	snake	stir	

tail	theirs	this	took	trust
tale	then	three	tool	truthful
tall	they	throne	tooth	trying
tan	they'll	throw	top	tub
tax	they've	Thursday	torches	tube
tearful	thick	tie	toss	Tuesday
ten	thimble	tightrope	tough	tug
tenth	thin	tile	tougher	turn
tested	thing	time	toughest	twelve
thank	think	tip	town	twenty
thankful	thinner	toe	toy	two
Thanksgiving	thinnest	tomorrow	trail	
that	third	tonight	train	
the	thirteen	to	tree	
their	thirty	too	true	

U

under	unfair	unlike	until	use
undo	United States	unload	up	used
uneasy	unjust	unlock	us	useful
uneven	unkind	unpack		

V

valentine	verb	verse	very

wait

waited

walk

walls

wanted

was

watch

watches

water

wax

waxes

we

weak

Wednesday

wee

well

went

were

weren't

we've

whale

what

wheat

when

where

which

while

whisper

white

who

whole

whose

why

will

win

wing

winter

wish

wishes

with

without

wonderful

won't

wood

wool

word

work

world

wouldn't

wow

write

X-Y-Z

x-ray

xylophone

yak

yam

yawn

yell

yellow

yes

you

your

you're

you've